AN INTRODUCTION

TO

COMPARATIVE PHILOLOGY

FOR CLASSICAL STUDENTS

AN INTRODUCTION

TO

COMPARATIVE PHILOLOGY

FOR CLASSICAL STUDENTS

BY

J. M. EDMONDS, M.A.,

LATE SCHOLAR OF JESUS COLLEGE, CAMBRIDGE,
ASSISTANT MASTER AT REPTON SCHOOL

CAMBRIDGE :
at the University Press
1906

CAMBRIDGE
UNIVERSITY PRESS

University Printing House, Cambridge CB2 8BS, United Kingdom

Cambridge University Press is part of the University of Cambridge.

It furthers the University's mission by disseminating knowledge in the pursuit of education, learning and research at the highest international levels of excellence.

www.cambridge.org
Information on this title: www.cambridge.org/9781107450714

© Cambridge University Press 1906

First published 1906
First paperback edition 2014

A catalogue record for this publication is available from the British Library

ISBN 978-1-107-45071-4 Paperback

PREFACE.

IN preparing pupils for Classical Scholarships I had
long felt the want of a book on Comparative Philology
adapted to their attainments, and now in compiling this
little Introduction I have tried to supply it. In aiming
at simplicity I have felt bound sometimes to sacrifice
completeness and omit details; but I hope that what I
have said will be found correct as far as it goes. The
theory of the Long 'Sonants' I have left alone. I have
given more space to the Consonants than to the Vowels.
English, especially the History of English, I have treated
with some neglect. When it is remembered that the
ordinary Sixth-Form boy knows little of Phonetics and
nothing of Old English, the reason of these and other
inconsistencies will, I hope, be clear. In smaller matters,
such as the division of words by hyphens and the marking
of quantities, I have sacrificed consistency to clearness.
In the case of forms only presumed to have existed, I have
omitted to denote this by an asterisk, and have preferred,
for instance, μέμηϙμεν to *mémṇmen as the supposed
original of μέμαμεν. Confusion with English spelling I
have tried to avoid by enclosing phonetic spelling, where
necessary, in round brackets, and by various expedients
such as printing t^h, p^h for the usual th, ph, and using w
and y for ṷ and ị. Readers acquainted with the alphabet

of the *Association phonétique internationale* will find some
of my phonetic symbols unfamiliar. But I felt that, in
the present state of the teaching of Phonetics, to adopt
that system would necessitate the multiplication of
symbols needing explanation to the majority of Classical
students; and in an elementary work of this kind the
fewer strange things the better.

The books I have laid chiefly under contribution are
those mentioned on page 201, but I am also indebted
to the writers of various articles in the *Encyclopaedia
Britannica*. Special thanks are due to Mr E. Abbott of
Jesus College for his great kindness in reading the whole
book in manuscript; to Mr H. J. Cape of the King's
School, Canterbury, for reading part of the proofs; to Mr
L. A. Burd of Repton for advice on several points; and to
Mr Giles for permission to use an illustration from his
article on Writing in the *Encyclopaedia Britannica*.
I may add that the drawings for the diagrams are nearly
all the work of my wife.

J. M. E.

REPTON,
September, 1906.

TABLE OF CONTENTS.

Note: *Inverted commas* denote meanings : thus, 'fire.'
        Italics   denote ordinary spelling : thus, *fire*.
        Round brackets   denote, where necessary, phonetic spelling:
                      thus, (fɐiǝ).

Errata: p. 80 ; 'About this time *j* began to be differentiated,' etc. :
            transpose this sentence to 4th line from bottom.

           p. 118, line 16 ; *Wycombe* would seem to be unhappily
           chosen ; according to Shore, *Origin of the Anglo-Saxon
           Race*, p. 266, it is a modern misspelling of *Wicham* or
           Wickham.

LIST OF DIAGRAMS.

Note: Nos. 2, 3 & 4 are adapted from Rippmann's *Elements of Phonetics.*

No. 5 is from the *Companion to Greek Studies.*

No. 8 is from the *Encyclopaedia Britannica,* Supplementary Volumes, under 'Writing.'

CHAPTER I.

LANGUAGE AND THE STUDY OF LANGUAGE.

Introductory—Acquiring our own language—Acquiring a foreign language—Province of Comparative Philology—Change—*Elements of Language*—Speech—Gesture—Feature—Tone of Voice—Pitch—Emphasis or Stress—Speed—*Origin of Speech*—Imitation of Animals—Interjections—Symbolism—Metaphor—*Differentiation in Language*—*Classification of Languages by Form*—Isolating—Agglutinative—Inflexional—Incorporating—Position of English—of French—of German—of Greek and Latin.

THE facts we learn in acquiring a language may be grouped under four heads:

(1)   Vocabulary, or words pure and simple,

(2)   Accidence, or the inflexions of nouns, verbs, etc.,

(3)   Syntax, or the arrangement of words in sentences,

(4)   Spelling, or the relation of the written to the spoken language.

A child acquiring his native language learns these facts

Acquiring our own language.
as a mass of associations. By imitating others he associates the sound-group *grass* with the thing 'grass,' and the sound-group *tree* with the thing 'tree'; the thing 'grass' and the thing 'tree' he associates together by means of a common characteristic, 'greenness,' that is, he acquires the abstract

E.   1

notion 'green,' and with this by imitation he associates the sound-group *green*. Simultaneously with the vocabulary, and in a similar way, he acquires the accidence and the syntax. The spelling-associations are acquired somewhat later.

When we learn a foreign language we acquire a new
Acquiring a foreign language.
set of associations. With the thing 'grass' we learn to associate the sound-group *herbe* as well as the sound-group *grass,* and with the notion 'green' we learn to associate the sound-group *vert* as well as the sound-group *green*. That is to say, we start with the mass of associations of which our native language consists, and gradually extend them in a new direction. The new associations we group mentally under the heading 'French,' and the process of acquiring associations becomes a comparison between English and French. We learn to write down the symbol-group 'herbe' to represent the sound-group *herbe,* and not to write 'airb' as we should if the sound-group belonged to the heading 'English[1].' We go through the same process with every new sound-group, and we gradually acquire a mass of associations such as *man = homme, is = est.* By a similar process we learn the inflexions *homme—hommes, est—sont,* and the sentences *l'homme est bon, les hommes sont bons.*

When we proceed to learn other foreign languages we begin to acquire fresh masses of associations, e.g. *man = Mann, man = homo, man = ἀνήρ, man = homme.* But we do not directly associate *Mann* with *homo,* or *ἀνήρ* with *homme*. For instance, we should find it difficult to translate a piece of German into French without first turning the German mentally into English. It is here that the

---

[1] In school teaching in England this order is frequently reversed, the spelling or look of a word being learnt before the pronunciation or sound.

province of Comparative Philology begins. It takes such

Province of
Comparative
Philology.

groups as *man — homme — Mann — homo —*
ἀνήρ and *he loves—il aime—er liebt—amat*
—ἐρᾷ, and compares the members of each
group. In short, Comparative Philology (or, as it is
sometimes called, Philology) deals with the phenomena
of Language as Natural Science deals with the phenomena
of Matter, i.e. it compares various phenomena, groups
them under heads according to their common characteristics, and deduces the laws or principles which govern
them. It is the business of Comparative Philology to
answer as far as possible such questions as Why does the
Frenchman say *il aime* where the Englishman says *he
loves*? Has the Englishman always said *he loves*? If
not, why not?

The Englishman has not always said *he loves*. In the

Change.

time of King Alfred (849—901) he said *he
lufath* (spelt 'lufaþ'). Similarly the French
il aime was once the Latin *ille amat*. Thus we see that
language changes; in other words, if an Englishman of
the time of Alfred were to come to life again he would
have at least as great difficulty in understanding one of
us as a Cockney has in understanding a Scotchman.

Before we deal with Change and its causes there are
several points to be discussed. First, as to the Elements
of Language.

Language is composed primarily of speech-sounds—

*Elements of
Language.*
(1) Speech.

vowels and consonants—formed by the organs
of the throat and mouth (see Chapter II.);
but it has many other elements. The phrase
'gesticulating foreigner' implies that foreigners when

(2) Gesture.

speaking employ Gesture, but that we do
not. It is true that gesture is less common

1—2

in English than in most other languages. We rarely shrug our shoulders or extend our hands while speaking. In church or in school, however, when we wish to avoid speaking, we can readily make known any simple want or intention in this way. Among some races, especially the lower races, gesture is far more widely employed, and in many cases enters directly into the spoken language. In Modern Greek οὐχί, 'no,' has degenerated into a mere parting of the lips accompanied by a tossing back of the head (the Classical ἀνανεύειν). In the Grebo language of West Africa *ni ne* means 'I do it' or 'you do it' according to the gesture of the speaker. Indeed, our own system of counting by tens—*twenty, thirty, forty*—proves that our linguistic ancestors indicated numbers by their fingers as savages do to this day. Under certain circumstances elaborate gesture-systems have been developed entirely independent of speech. Among the North American Indians, owing to the great variety of languages, a common gesture-system is often employed, with which conversation can be carried on. Deaf-mutes have been known to develop a language of the same kind. We may note here that an Englishman who never employs gesture while speaking at home, on going abroad resorts to it frequently. This is partly, no doubt, owing to unconscious imitation of the inhabitants, but largely, too, because he feels that his imperfect pronunciation of the language requires help.

Another element of language is Expression of Feature.

(3) Feature.   Just as we have learnt to associate a certain emotion with the noise we call laughing, so certain emotions such as pride, disgust, humility, shame, anger, have come to be connected with certain expressions of face, and thus an angry word is always accompanied by an angry look. This association of the expression of face

with speech is so deeply rooted that in the dark we imagine it accompanying the spoken word. In this we are of course guided by the Tone of Voice, which we may call the fourth element in language. Even without the help of the facial expression it is not hard to distinguish a sarcastic laugh from a merry one. Our colloquial 'Irishism,' 'Don't look at me in that tone of voice,' acknowledges the close connexion between tone and feature. Indeed, it is not uncommon among intimates to express interest, interrogation, surprise, etc., by tone alone, i.e. by voice-murmur with the closed lips. Such symbol-groups as 'h'm,' 'humph,' are intended to express this on paper. When we talk of 'speaking kindly' to a dog, we know it is the tone of voice rather than the words which he understands. For this reason many men when calling a small animal will speak in falsetto.

(4) Tone of Voice.

Other elements of language are Musical Pitch, Emphasis or Stress, and Speed of Utterance. These are exemplified in such phrases as '*Ever* so far away,' 'I can't *tell* you how much I enjoyed it,' 'Then with a *terrific roar* the whole vessel was blown into the air.' In the last instance the noise and terror of the explosion, as well as the climax of the story, are indicated by the emphasis, the high pitch, and the slowness of utterance, of the two words in italics. In a sentence like 'I can't walk there,' the emphasis may be placed on any one of the four syllables with a different meaning in each case. The importance of these latter elements of speech is seen in reading aloud. To produce the full effect intended by the writer of the book the reader must guess the tone and speed of every sentence and the pitch and emphasis of every syllable; for this is more than the most scientifically accurate alphabet could convey.

(5) Pitch.
(6) Emphasis.
(7) Speed.

These subsidiary elements of language—Gesture, Expression of Feature, Tone of Voice, Pitch, Emphasis, and Speed of Utterance—occupy an important place in the languages of modern savages, and doubtless did so in the early stages of the languages of civilisation. The more highly-developed a language becomes, that is, the more perfect a vehicle of thought, the less reliance it places on these subsidiary elements. As we saw above, speech begins in the infant with associations, first, between sounds and things ('trees,' 'grass'), secondly, between sounds and notions or ideas ('green'). It is probable that it *Origin of Speech.* originated in the first instance in a similar way. The infant imitates its parents and others. What did the first speaker imitate? How did the association between the original sound-groups and the things they expressed come into existence?

Doubtless many of the first words were Imitations of the cries of animals such as *moo, baa,* *Imitation of animals.* uttered either for amusement, as children utter them now, or for purposes of decoying. Then the sound-group *moo* would be used to modify a gesture, such as that of pointing, to explain what kind of animal was pointed at. The stage of using a sound-group to modify a gesture or expression of the face was probably a long one, but a time must have come when a savage wished to express 'there is an ox' in the dark, where gesture and expression of face would be useless; and thus *moo* alone would be employed as a sentence-word with this meaning.

At a very early period in his history[1] man could doubtless express his feelings in a limited *Interjections.* way by various Interjections, just as a dog

[1] The earliest stages of the growth of Language were probably contemporary with the 'monkey stage' of human development.

can either bark or growl, and a hen either cackle or cluck, according to circumstances. Thus *ugh*, accompanied by suitable pointing-gestures, might mean 'I have the toothache,' or 'he has sprained his ankle.' After a long use of these primitive methods of communication, the savage, we may suppose, began to combine such a sound-group as *moo* with such a sound-group as *ugh*. 'There-is-an-ox there-is-pain' would be the result. Accompanied by suitable gestures this could mean 'I am going to stab that ox with this spear,' or 'Let us come and stab that ox with our spears,' or even 'They have killed this ox with their spears.' Once such combinations had become possible, sentence-words such as *moo* ('there-is-an-ox') and *ugh* ('there-is-pain') would gradually develop into true words, the one meaning 'ox' and the other 'stab' or 'kill.' These could be used in various combinations.

Another likely origin of words is Symbolism, such as

Symbolism.   the act of sucking-in the breath between the upper teeth and the lower lip to denote either drinking or sweetness to the taste. The Latin *bibere* may be *originally* a 'baby-word' of this kind. To this day we often denote the idea 'delicious' in this way. We may note here the symbolism seen in Vowel-Contrast. For instance, the Javanese say *iki* for 'this,' *ika* for 'that (near),' and *iku* for 'that (yonder),' and even the Greeks, when they wished to emphasise the nearness of a thing, changed τόδε to τοδί. In both cases degrees of distance are indicated by variety of vowels. The same thing is used to indicate sex. Thus in Finnish *ukko* is an old man, *akka* an old woman; indeed, such a phenomenon as *bonum—bonam* may be referred historically to the same principle[1].

---

[1] For the connexion between Vowel Gradation and Musical Pitch see Chapter VII.

It should be borne in mind in discussing the probable origin of speech that, to become the fixed expression of any particular idea, a word would have to be employed constantly by a number of persons to one another and to stand tests such as ease of pronunciation (organic) and distinctiveness (acoustic). It was a case of the survival of the fittest.

We have still to discuss a most important element in the formation of speech,—Metaphor. This is an obvious way of expressing the hitherto unknown in terms of the known. When the native Australians first became acquainted with books they called them *mūyūm*, 'mussels,' because they open and shut in a similar way. The Basuto word for a fly, *ntsi-ntsi*, which is obviously imitative of buzzing[1], has been extended by metaphor to mean a courtier, i.e. one who buzzes round his chief. The history of three words for tobacco-pipe, *chibouk*, *calumet*, and our *pipe*, points to a similar origin. *Chibouk* comes from Central Asia, where it meant originally a herdsman's flute. *Calumet* in the dialect of Normandy (from Latin *calamus*) is the name for a shepherd's pipe, and was applied to the smoking-instrument of the Red Indians by the early colonists of Canada. Our *pipe* was once used with the same meaning. In the translation of the Psalms we read 'Praise him upon the strings and pipe.' We still speak of the pipes of an organ. A similar extension of association by metaphor gave us such words as *drain-pipe, wind-pipe*. The history of the word *junketing* is a case in point. From the Latin *iuncus*, 'a reed,' came Late Latin *iuncata*, 'cheese made in a reed-basket,' which in Italian appears as *giuncata*, 'cream-cheese,' and in French as *joncade*, 'curds-and-whey,' whence we have

Metaphor.

---

[1] Cf. Mod. Greek τσίτσικος, a cricket.

the English *junket*; from the *junketing*-parties where
this delicacy was eaten we get the noun *junketing* meaning 'merry-making.' To take another instance, *peculiar*
comes through French from the Latin *peculiaris*, originally the adjective of *peculium*, a slave's private hoard;
this again is a diminutive of *pecunia*, 'money,' once 'pro-
perty' of any kind, earlier 'live-stock' from *pecus*, 'cattle';
in Sanskrit[1] *paçu* means 'cattle,' and is formed from *paç*, 'to
fasten up' (Latin *pango*, Greek πήγνυμι), the original meaning being doubtless 'domestic' as opposed to 'wild' cattle.
If we wonder at the fewness of such self-expressive words
as *cuckoo, buzz, hiss, pompom* in a language like our own,
compared with the enormous number of such words as *go,
black, man, never,* whose meaning is merely traditional,
we have only to consider such extensions of meaning as
these.

We have indicated briefly the Elements of Language
Differentia-   (in the widest sense), and the probable Origin
tion in   and Development of Speech (or Language
Language.   in the narrow sense). We shall now discuss
the causes of Differentiation in Language, i.e. the split-
ting up into dialects. These causes are mainly local.

Let us imagine a small village-community where,
roughly speaking, everyone spoke to everyone else every
day. So long as the conditions remained the same, the
necessities of mutual intelligibility would preserve the
language of the villagers from change, or if it did change
the changes would, in the long run, be common to all
the inhabitants. But suppose, under pressure of in-
creasing population, decreasing fertility of the soil, or
catastrophes such as floods and landslips, the community
spread further and further, till natural boundaries such

[1] For the connexion between Latin and Sanskrit see Chapter v.

as rivers and mountains divided the speakers of the original language into new and distinct communities. Not only might names have to be found for new objects, but changes in the forms and uses of words (owing, e.g., to laziness or to defective imitation in infants) would not necessarily, under different circumstances, follow the same lines. Between some of the villages communication, in varying degrees, might be kept up. The divergence in dialect would probably be inversely proportional to the ease of inter-communication. Thus, if we call the original village A and its successive offshoots *in any one direction* B, C, and D, the chances of remaining mutually intelligible would be greater in the case of A and B than in the case of A and C or of A and D. Similarly the dialects of C and D would have more elements in common than those of B and D. B and C might have the same *number* of elements in common as C and D, but these would not necessarily be *the same* elements. If owing to any cause B or C moved from their intermediate position, the chances of A and D becoming mutually unintelligible would be greatly increased.

We have imagined our community as already so far advanced in civilisation as to dwell for long periods in one district. It will be understood that in the case of nomad or wandering peoples the circumstances would be still more favourable to differentiation.

(The causes of Change in language are discussed more fully in Chapter VI.)

The languages of the world may be classified in many *Classification of Languages according to Form.* ways, e.g. living and dead, written and un-written; they may be classified according to their descent, or according to their form.

According to their Form languages may be classified under three heads:

(1) Isolating (also called Radical and Monosyllabic),

(2) Agglutinative,

(3) Inflexional.

In Isolating languages, such as Chinese, there is no inflexion (e.g. *amo—amas, man—men*).
(1) Isolating.
A word never undergoes modification, but grammatical relations such as object and subject are expressed partly by the order of the words (as in English *Tom hit Jack* contrasted with *Jack hit Tom*), partly by the use of particles. Such languages make a large use of Tone in distinguishing words otherwise identical (see Chapter III.).

Agglutinative languages, such as Turkish, stand halfway between Isolating languages on the one side and Inflexional languages on the other.
(2) Agglutinative.
They express grammatical relations by prefix or suffix; but the sounds so employed are always clearly distinguishable from the word they qualify. In an Agglutinative language all words are modified as the English *care, believe*, in *care-less-ness, un-believ-able*, where *-less, -ness, un-, -able*, though without meaning when they stand alone[1], are all clearly distinguishable. In such languages words can be separated from their modifying syllables and yet remain intact—'word' and 'stem' are in them interchangeable terms.

In Inflexional languages, such as the languages with which in this book we are chiefly concerned, the stem is a mere abstraction, existing perhaps in the mind of the speaker but
(3) Inflexional.

[1] I.e. we cannot, under any circumstances we like, use *less* to mean 'without,' or *un* to mean 'not.'

never used in actual speaking[1], while the prefixes and suffixes have a far less distinct meaning than in Agglutinative languages. Thus in the Latin *hominis -is* gives the meaning 'of,' and in *homines -es* gives the meaning 'more than one,' but 'of men' is not expressed by *homin-es-is* or *homin-is-es*, as it would be in an Agglutinative language. Moreover in languages of this class stems are modified internally, as *man—men*, πείθειν—πιθεῖν.

To these three great classes a fourth may be added known as Incorporating. Such languages are

(4) Incorporating.

really an extreme type of the Inflexional class. In the Basque language of the Pyrenees inflexions are provided for all possible combinations of pronouns with verbs, e.g. 'I-go-to-him,' 'Let-them-bring-her-to-us.'

It will be seen that each of these classes shades off into the next. Between Agglutinative and Inflexional, particularly, it is hard to draw the line. It is probable that to some extent these classes mark stages of development, and that all Inflexional languages must once have been Isolating and have passed through an Agglutinative stage.

The question, to which class does English belong? is not easy to answer. By descent it is

Position of English.

Inflexional. Old English (or Anglo-Saxon) has as elaborate systems of declension as Greek or Latin. In Modern English, however, the prepositions *of, to, by*, etc., have almost entirely taken the place of case-suffixes, and what Latin expresses by tense-suffixes and person-suffixes we express by auxiliaries and pronouns (e.g. *illis, to them* ; *amabo, I will love*). Our inflexion is practically confined to the following:

---

[1] Strictly, this could be said only of languages *entirely* inflexional; in Greek, λόγε the vocative and λέγε the imperative are stems without suffix or other modification.

In nouns:

>   the -*s* of the plural (*cats*),
>   the -*s* of the possessive (*cat's*, *cats'*).

In adjectives:

>   the -*er* of the comparative (*high-er*),
>   the -*est* of the superlative (*high-est*).

In verbs :

>   the auxiliaries (*am*, *are*; *have*, *has*),
>   the 'strong' verbs (*sing*, *sang*, *sung*),
>   the past tense and participle (*stay*, *stay-ed*),
>   the present participle and verbal (*go*, *go-ing*),
>   the third person singular of the present tense
>   (*love*, *love-s*).

Now though the prepositions *of*, *to*, *by*, etc., are *written* apart from the word they qualify, in *pronunciation* there is no break. They are virtually prefixes; and as the word they qualify remains unmodified their use has every claim to be considered an Agglutinative element. On the other hand, whole sentences may be composed in English of unmodified words which depend for their meaning on their order alone, e.g. *Dick hit Tom* contrasted with *Tom hit Dick*, *Hit Dick*, *Tom*, and *Hit Tom*, *Dick*. In such sentences English is Isolating. The same principle is seen in such collocations as *The Cambridge University Rugby Union Football Club*, as well as in the compounds *railway, tea-cup, garden-roller, county-council*, with which they are structurally identical[1]. But

---

[1] An interesting example of the tendency of English to become Agglutinative is seen in the -*s* of the possessive. We can now say *With the Bishop and Mrs Smith's best wishes*, where the '*s* belongs to the Bishop as well as to Mrs Smith; and it is quite usual to speak of *the Member for Canterbury's speech*, or even *the man from Birmingham's proposal*, where the suffix '*s* is separated from its noun-stem by a prepositional phrase. Some day we may say *the man that hit me's fist*. This *s* was once as truly an integral part of the noun as the -*is* of the Latin *honoris*.

though the inflexions of English are nowadays few, they still form an essential part of the language. This being so, Modern English may be described as an Inflexional language which has developed both Isolating and Agglutinative characteristics.

In French, nouns are less inflected even than in
French.   English, but the verbs still show elaborate
inflexions (e.g. *aime, aimons, aimez, aimerai, aimasse*).

In German, while the facility with which compounds
German.   like *Aufnahmefähigkeit* ('eligibility') are
formed, points to agglutination, the noun-inflexions are a marked feature of the language.

Greek and Latin are good types of the Inflexional
class, though even in them such phrases as
Greek and
Latin.   καταβάλλειν, *ad oppidum*, show an Agglutinative element, while 'indeclinable' words
like δέκα, *frugi*, are distinctly Isolating in character.

CHAPTER II.

THE MECHANISM OF SPEECH, AND THE CLASSIFICATION OF SOUNDS.

The Apparatus of Speech — Larynx — Vocal Chords — Glottis — 'Indeterminate Vowel'—Pharynx—Epiglottis—Tongue—Soft Palate—Nose—Mouth—Rounding the Lips—Breath, Voice, and Whisper—Examples of Consonants—Vowel and Consonant defined and distinguished—*Classification of Consonants*—(i) by Form—Spirants—Stops—Nasals—Liquids—(ii) by Place—Velars — Palatals — Cerebrals — Alveolars and Dentals—Inter-dentals — Labiodentals — Labials—Table of Consonants—(i) Breathed—(ii) Voiced — Uvula-Stops—Breathed Nasals and Liquids—*q* and *k*—*Classification of Vowels*—Difference between (χ) and (*i*)—Vowel Positions—(i) Vertical—(ii) Horizontal—Rounding—Narrow and Wide—Scheme of Vowels—*Other Sounds* —Nasalised Vowels—'Sonants'—Diphthongs — Triphthongs—Glides—The Aspirate—Aspirated Stops.

IN order to understand the laws of Change in language we must have a clear idea, first, of the way in which speech-sounds are produced, and, secondly, of their classification.

We can produce sound either by in-breathing or by out-breathing; custom and convenience have decided, for purposes of speech, on the use of out-breathing[1]. The

[1] We sometimes, however, say *no* by breathing inwards, generally with a shake of the head.

course of the breath from the lungs to the lips is as
follows.   It is driven, by the contraction of the ribs and
Larynx.   the diaphragm, up the windpipe (in the front
                   of the neck) to the Larynx or Adam's apple.
Here the sound is as it were formed in the rough.   The

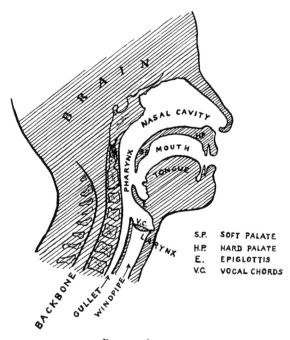

S.P.   SOFT PALATE
H.P.   HARD PALATE
E.   EPIGLOTTIS
V.C.   VOCAL CHORDS

DIAGRAM 1.

Larynx is an oval box of cartilage or gristle, across which
                   are stretched the two Vocal Chords.   These
Vocal Chords.   are elastic ligaments, roughly semi-circular
in shape, which by muscular action can be made to expand

either in length or in width with the following different effects:

(1) They close together entirely as in 'holding the breath,'

(2) They open wide as in ordinary breathing,

(3) They allow the breath to pass through a narrow slit, which causes them to vibrate like the string of a violin and so produce sound,

(4) They lengthen or shorten themselves (i.e. loosen or tighten themselves) to lower or raise the musical pitch of the sound (just as the longest and loosest strings of a piano give the lowest notes)[1],

(5) They allow the breath to pass through a narrow slit, without, however, causing them to vibrate—this is known as 'whisper.'

The slit or opening between the two Vocal Chords is called the Glottis.

Glottis.

Now let us suppose that the narrow slit has been formed. If no further modification is made by the parts of the throat and mouth above the Glottis, the sound which emerges from the mouth is that roughly represented in English as *er*, i.e. the sound we make when we hesitate for a word in a speech.

Indeterminate Vowel.

This sound is known as the 'Indeterminate (i.e. unmodified) Vowel' and is indicated in this book by the symbol (ə).

If, on the other hand, some other sound is required, simultaneously with the vibration of the Vocal Chords a modification is made in the size and shape of the Pharynx. This is the cavity beyond the back of the mouth, forming the upper extremity of the

[1] The different modifications of the Glottis which produce 'chest-voice,' 'head-voice,' and 'falsetto' respectively, do not concern us here.

E.   2

Gullet or food-passage. The passage between the Pharynx
and the Larynx is open during the formation of speech-
sound, but closed in the act of swallowing by a kind of

Epiglottis.

valve or flap called the Epiglottis. (When
we draw in our breath with our mouth full
of food a crumb is apt to 'go down the wrong way,' i.e. to
get into the Larynx or voice-box instead of into the Gullet
or food-passage. To clear the obstruction we cough, i.e.
we close the Vocal Chords and open them with a jerk,
thus allowing a sudden jet of breath to escape.)

The size and shape of the Pharynx is regulated (1) by

Tongue.
Soft Palate.

the lower and hinder part of the Tongue;
(2) by the Soft Palate or Velum, the soft
hinder part of the roof of the mouth. The
various modifications produce the various Vowel-sounds.

Nose and
Mouth.

From the Pharynx the breath can get out by
one or both of two passages, the Nose and
the Mouth. If the sound required is an
ordinary vowel such as *ah* (ā), the Soft Palate closes,
or nearly closes[1], the passage from the Pharynx to the
Nose. If, on the other hand, it is to be a Nasalised Vowel
as in the French *son, sain*, the passage to the Nose remains entirely open as well as the Mouth. Vowel-sounds

Rounding
the Lips.

can be further modified by the Rounding or
pouting of the Lips as in *oo* (e.g. *boot*).

So much for the production of the Vowel-sounds.

Consonants can be either Breathed, Voiced, or

Breath, Voice,
and Whisper.

Whispered, that is to say, in the production
of them the Glottis can be either (1) wide
open, (2) closed to a narrow slit *with* vibration
of the Vocal Chords, or (3) closed to a narrow slit *without*

[1] In the case of singers, particularly, it remains partly open, thus
securing for the sound additional 'resonance' or ring.

vibration of the Vocal Chords. But the most important
variation is produced by the method and extent of the
obstruction caused to the passage of the breath by

> the Soft Palate,
> the Hard Palate,
> the Tongue,
> the Teeth-Roots or Alveoli,
> the Teeth,

and the Lips,

acting separately or in various combinations.

Thus in the formation of the consonant d (pronounced,
of course, not as *dee* but as d'), (1) the Vocal
Chords vibrate; (2) the Soft Palate closes,
or nearly closes, the Nose-passage; and (3) the Tongue
closes the Mouth-passage by touching with its tip the
Roots of the upper front Teeth: d may therefore be
described as the *voiced* Alveolar Stop.

d.

If the organs are in the same positions save that the
Glottis is wide open so that the Vocal Chords
do not vibrate, the result is t, which may be
described as the *breathed* (or unvoiced) Alveolar Stop. If
again the organs are in the same positions as
in pronouncing d, save that the Nose-passage
is left wide open by the Soft Palate, the result is the
ordinary n, which is the voiced Nasal Alveolar Stop.

t.

n.

A Vowel, then, may be defined as Voice (i.e. vibration
of the Vocal Chords) modified in the Pharynx
by the Tongue and the Soft Palate, but *without audible friction* (which would make it a
Consonant); while a Consonant is the result
either of audible friction (as s) or of the
stopping of the breath in some part of the Mouth or
Throat (as t). In a Vowel the action of the Glottis is

Vowel and
Consonant
Defined and
Distin-
guished.

2—2

a primary element, in a Consonant merely secondary; in
a Vowel the configuration of the Throat and Mouth is of
secondary importance only, in a Consonant it is essential[1].

In describing the production of sounds we dealt with
Classification   the Vowels first, but as the Classification of
of Con-   Vowels presents the greater difficulties, we
sonants.   shall now reverse the order and take the
Classification of Consonants.

Consonants may be classified (i) according to Form;
(ii) according to Place, i.e. place of formation.

(i) By Form there are four classes:

(1) Spirants or Open Consonants: in these the
Spirants.   passage (e.g. between the Tongue and the
                   Teeth-Roots, as in *s, z*) is simply narrowed,
not entirely closed (this would make it a Stop; see
Diagram 2, where three typical positions of the Tongue
are shown in section).

(2) Stops or Shut Consonants (sometimes called
Stops.   Mutes, as being, strictly, not sounds but
                'silences'): in these the passage (e.g. be-
tween the Tongue and the Teeth-Roots, as in *t, d*) is
entirely closed.

(3) Nasals or Nose Consonants : in these the Mouth-
Nasals.   passage (e.g. between the Tongue and the
                 Teeth-Roots, as in *n*) is entirely closed, the
breath escaping through the Nose.

(4) Liquids or   i. Divided Consonants: these are the
Liquids : *l*.   different varieties of *l*; the middle of the
                        passage (e.g. between the Tongue and
                    [1] Sweet, *Primer of Phonetics*, p. 30.

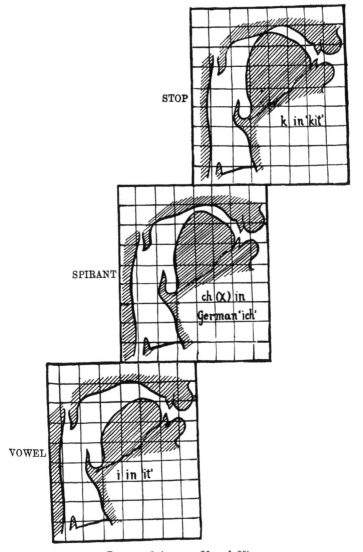

STOP

k in 'kit'

SPIRANT

ch (χ) in German 'ich'

VOWEL

i in 'it'

DIAGRAM 2 (see pp. 20 and 29).

the Teeth-Roots, as in the English *l*) is closed, while one
or both sides remain open to the passage of breath.

r.

         ii. Trilled Consonants: these are the
different varieties of *r*; they are really a
variety of Spirants; they consist in the vibration of the flexible parts of the Mouth either against
one another (e.g. the Lips, as in the interjection *brr!*) or
against a firm part (e.g. the Tongue against the Teeth-
Roots, as in the Scotch trilled *r*). In the English *r*, as
in *run*, no trill takes place, the tip of the Tongue merely
going into position for a trill which never comes.

    (ii) By Place there are seven main classes:

    (1) Velar or Back Consonants (also called Guttural):

Velars.

these are formed by the *root* of the Tongue
and the Soft Palate (or Velum). Instances
are: the *k*- or *q*-sound before such vowels as *ah*, *aw* (ā, ɔ);
the *ch* (written phonetically x) of German *ach*; and the
ng (ŋ) of *sing*. The first of these is a Velar Stop, the
second a Velar Spirant, and the third a Velar Nasal.

    (2) Palatal or Front Consonants: these are formed

Palatals.

by the *middle* of the Tongue and the Hard
Palate. Instances are: the *k*-sound before
such vowels as *e* in *ken* or *i* in *kin*; the *ch* (written
phonetically χ) of German *ich*; and the *gn* (ñ) of French
ligne. The first of these is a Palatal Stop, the second a
Palatal Spirant, and the third a Palatal Nasal.

    (3) Cerebral Consonants: these are formed by the

Cerebrals.

blade (or part immediately behind the tip)
of the Tongue and the front of the Hard
Palate, as *sh* (ṣ) in *she*, which is a Cerebral Spirant.

(4)   Alveolar or Teeth-Root Consonants (also called
                    Dental[1]): these are formed by the tip of
Alveolars and   the Tongue and the *roots* of the upper Teeth.
Dentals.
                    Instances are: *t* as in *ten*; *s* as in *sun*; and
n as in *not*. The first of these is an Alveolar Stop, the
second an Alveolar Spirant, and the third an Alveolar
Nasal.

(5)   Interdental Consonants: these are formed by the
                    tip of the Tongue and the *tips* of the front
Interdentals.   Teeth, as *th* (þ) in English *thin*, which is an
Interdental Spirant.

(6)   Labiodental or Lip-Teeth Consonants: these are
                    formed by the upper Teeth and the lower
Labiodentals.   Lip, as *f* in English *fat*, which is a Labiodental Spirant.

(7)   Labial or Lip Consonants: these are formed by
                    the upper and lower Lips. Instances are:
Labials.   *p* as in English *pit*, and *m* as in *man*, the
first being a Labial Stop and the second a Labial
Nasal.

Besides its classification according to Form and Place
a Consonant can belong, as has been explained above, to
one of three classes according as it is Breathed, Voiced, or
Whispered. It is sufficient for our present purpose if we
distinguish Breathed and Voiced. In the following Table
of Consonants it should be understood that most of the
blank spaces could be filled up by instances from various
less familiar languages and dialects.

---

[1] The true Dental is heard in the French *t*, as in *ton*, compared with
the Alveolar English *t*, as in *ten*.

1. BREATHED:

| | SPIRANT | STOP[1] | NASAL | LIQUID | |
				DIVIDED	TRILLED
LABIAL	wh *where,* *twenty*	p pʰ *pen uphold*[2]	—	—	—
LABIO-DENTAL	f *fan*	—	—	—	—
INTER-DENTAL	þ *thin*	—	—	—	—
ALVEOLAR (OR DENTAL)	s *so*	t tʰ *ten at-home*[2]	—	—	—
CEREBRAL	ṣ (or *sh*) *fish*	—	—	—	—
PALATAL	χ[3] Germ. *ich*	k kʰ *king inkhorn*[2]	—	—	—
VELAR	x Germ. *ach*	q qʰ *queen —*	—	—	—

[1] For the Aspirated Stops see below under the Aspirate.
[2] Only approximate; see below under the Aspirate.
[3] Not, of course, the *Greek* χ, which was (kʰ).

CONSONANTS.

2. VOICED:

	SPIRANT	STOP[1]		NASAL	LIQUID	
					DIVIDED	TRILLED
LABIAL	w *were*	b *bet*	b^h *abhor*[2]	m *am*	—	r Exclamation spelt *brr!*
LABIO-DENTAL	v *van*	—		—	—	—
INTER-DENTAL	đ *then*	—		—	—	—
ALVEOLAR (OR DENTAL)	z *zeal, raise*	d *den*	d^h *adhere*[2]	n *in*	l *let*	r *run* Scotch and N. Eng. Dial. (Standard Eng. is untrilled)
CEREBRAL	ẓ (or *zh*) *azure, rouge*	—		—	—	r S.W. English Dialects
PALATAL	y *you*	g *leg*	g^h *leg-hit*[2]	ñ *ligne* (Fr.) *señor* (Sp.)	λ *gl* in It. *degli*	—
VELAR	ʒ Germ. *Lage*	g̣ —	g̣^h —	ŋ (or *ng*) *sing, sink*	—	r Germ. *Rat*, Fr. *rat*, Northumbrian 'burr'

[1] For the Aspirated Stops see below under the Aspirate.
[2] Only approximate; see below under the Aspirate.

One species of English consonant is not classified
Uvula-Stops   above, the Uvula-Stops. Instances are the
tn,   breathed Alveolar Uvula-Stop *tn* in *bitten*,
dn,   and the corresponding voiced Alveolar Uvula-
Stop *dn* in *bidden*. These are formed by placing the
Tongue in the position for *t* or *d* and then 'exploding'
the breath through the Nose by means of the Uvula (or
end of the Velum), instead of through the Mouth by
means of the Tongue. The corresponding *kn*
kn, kn̄,   is sometimes heard in such words as *bacon*,
pm, bm.   becoming (kn̄) before *g* as in *You c'n gó*.
Similarly, we have *pm* and *bm* in such words as *cap'm*
(generally spelt 'cap'n,' for *captain*).

As an instance of a *breathed* Nasal we may add the
kn in *know*, which was pronounced as a
Breathed   breathed *n*, or (nh), 150 years ago, though the
Nasals and
Liquids.   word is now identical with *no*. Even in
Modern English, when *n* adjoins a breathed
spirant (e.g. *sneer*) it is said by some phoneticians to
lose its voice (i.e. become breathed) in part; similarly *m*
(e.g. *smear*), and the liquids *l* (e.g. *play*) and *r* (e.g. *pray*).

It should be noted here that the English *ch* in *church*
is simply a combination of *t* and *sh* (ṣ), and
English *ch, j*
or 'soft' *g*.   English *j* or 'soft' *g* in *judge* a combination
of *d* and *zh* (ẓ), while the English *x*
(contrast the breathed Velar Spirant (x) = *ch* in Germ.
English *x*.   *ach*) is a superfluous letter, being simply *ks*
as in *fix* or *gz* as in *exact*.

It will be noticed that we have given no examples
above of the sounds *g* and *gh*. These sounds,
g and *gh*.   which will be referred to in a subsequent
chapter, bear the same relation to *q* and *qh* as *g* and *gh*
do to *k* and *kh*. The distinction between *q* and *k* is that

q is produced further back in the throat ; *q* is heard in
English before *w* (spelt *u*), as in *queen*, and
q and *k*.   also before certain vowels, e.g. *aw* (ɔ) as
in *caw*, and *o* as in *cot*. The difference may be felt by
comparing *king* (kiɒ) with *kong* (qoɒ).

Diagram 3 (on the next page) is intended to illustrate
the above classification of Consonants. It represents in
three sections (from left to right):

> the back of the Throat,
> the Uvula and Soft Palate,
> the back of the Hard Palate,
> the front of the Hard Palate,
> the Teeth-Roots,
> the Upper Teeth,
> and the Upper Lip.

The black dots represent approximately the point of contact or friction between the tip (or other parts) of the
Tongue and the Palate, Teeth-Roots, and Upper Teeth,
except in the case of the Labiodentals and Labials, where
the place of the Tongue is taken by the Lower Lip. The
symbol of each sound is given beneath the black dot where
contact or friction takes place, the Breathed above the
Voiced. The dotted lines denote approximately the passage
of the breath during the pronunciation of the various Consonants. The Tongue and the lower part of the Mouth
are not represented.

We defined a Vowel as Voice (i.e. vibration of the
Vocal Chords) modified in the Pharynx by
Classification
of Vowels.   the Tongue and the Soft Palate, but without
Difference   audible friction. When we form the Palatal
between (χ)   Spirant (χ)[1] (*ch* in German *ich*), the breath
and (i).   passes through a narrow passage between the

---

[1] Not, of course, the *Greek* χ, which was (kʰ).

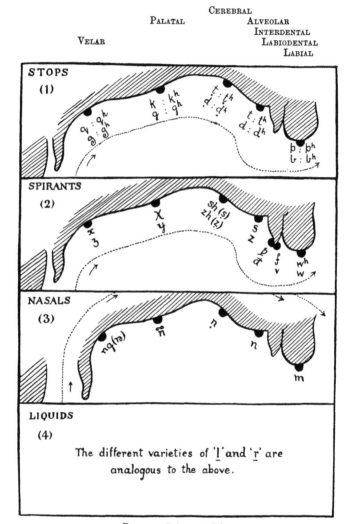

DIAGRAM 3 (see p. 27).

middle of the Tongue and the Hard Palate, and there is audible friction. Now if we lower the Tongue slightly from this position, and at the same time cause the Vocal Chords to vibrate, there is Voice, but no audible friction; we are producing the vowel in *it*. The Tongue is still arched towards the Hard Palate but not so high as before (see Diagram 2 on page 21). Again, if we pronounce the vowel *aw* (ɔ) in *law*, we find that the Tongue sinks to the bottom of the Mouth (see Diagram 4). Lastly, if we pronounce the vowel *ah* (ā) in *father*, we find the Tongue in an intermediate position. (The changes of position may be easily studied in a mirror which faces the light.)

Vowel Positions: *i* in *it*,

aw, *ah*.

HIGH   LOW

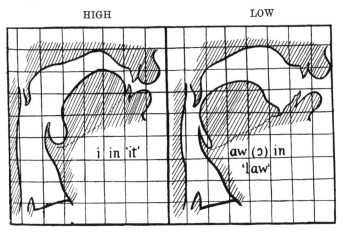

DIAGRAM 4. [This also illustrates FRONT and BACK.]

Thus, in the formation of the Vowels, we have three Vertical positions of the Tongue, *Low*, *Mid*, and *High*.

(1) Vertical Positions.

We have also three Horizontal positions. If we pronounce the *i* in *it*, then the word *err* (ə̄), and
(2) Horizontal Positions. then the *ah* (ā) in *father*, we find that the
Tongue moves horizontally from one position
to the next, being furthest forward at (i) and furthest
back at (ā) (see Diagram 4 on the previous page). These
three Horizontal positions are called *Front, Mixed,* and
Back (or Palatal, Gutturo-Palatal, and Velar or Guttural).

If we combine these two classifications, Vertical and
Horizontal, we have nine principal positions.

Now each of these nine vowel-sounds can be still
further modified. If we take the mirror again and pronounce the *i* in *it* and then the *aw* (ɔ) in *law*, we notice
that the corners of the Mouth in the first case are wide
apart in an unconstrained position, and in the second case
are slightly drawn together. This drawing together of the
(3) Rounding. corners of the Mouth is called Rounding (or
Labialisation), and all vowels can be classified as *Round* or *Unround*.

Lastly, if we contrast the *aw* (ɔ) in *law* with the *o* in
(4) Narrow and Wide. *not*, we find that in the first case the Tongue
is more tense and the surface more convex
than in the second. This distinction is known as that of
Narrow (tense and convex) and *Wide* (loose and concave).

To recapitulate, we have these four modes of classifying
the vowels:

> Low, Mid, or High,
> Front, Mixed, or Back,
> Round or Unround,
> Narrow or Wide,

making a total of thirty-six varieties. Still further distinctions, into which we need not enter, bring the number
to seventy-two[1].

The following scheme will suffice for our present purpose:

[1] See Sweet, *Primer of Phonetics.*

TABLE OF PRINCIPAL VOWELS.

			LOW	MID	HIGH
FRONT	NAR-ROW	Round	—	(*ö*) *in Fr.* peu	(*ü*) *in Fr.* pur
		Unrd.	(*e*) first element of diphthong in *fair*	(*e*) *in Fr.* été	(*i*) *in Fr.* si
	WIDE	Round	—	—	—
		Unrd.	(æ)[1] in *man*	(e) in *men*, and first element of diphthong in *say*	(i) in *bit*, and first element of diphthong in *fear* and when long of that in *see*
MIXED	NAR-ROW	Round	—	—	—
		Unrd.	(ə̄) in *sir*	—	—
	WIDE	Round	—	—	—
		Unrd.	(a) first element of diphthong in *how*	(ə) in the sof*a*	—
BACK	NAR-ROW	Round	(ɔ) in *law*	(o) *in Fr.* beau	(ū) in *cruel*
		Unrd.	—	(ɐ) in *butt*, *come*, and first element of diphthong in *high*	—
	WIDE	Round	(o) in *not*, and first element of diphthong in *boy*	—	(u) in *put*
		Unrd.	(ɒ) *in Fr.* pas	(ā) in *father*	—

[1] This symbol is not to be confused with the Latin diphthong *ae* which is sometimes so written.

From the above scheme it will be seen that we have
Eleven¹ Simple Vowels in English, namely those in the
following words: l*a*w, n*o*t, b*u*tt, f*a*ther, cr*ue*l, p*u*t, s*i*r, th*e*
s*o*fa, m*a*n, m*e*n, b*i*t. The nine¹ other so-called Vowels,
exemplified in b*oy*, s*o*, h*igh*, t*oo*, h*ow*, f*air*, s*ay*, f*ear*,
s*ee*, are Diphthongs (see below).

Besides Vowels and Consonants there are several other
Other Sounds. classes of sounds, which we shall notice in the
following order: Nasalised Vowels, 'Sonants,'
Diphthongs, Glides, and the Aspirate.

In the production of ordinary Vowels the passage
Nasalised Vowels. to the Nose is closed or nearly closed, the
breath escaping through the Mouth. If,
however, the Nose-passage remains wide
open, so that the breath escapes both by the Nose and
by the Mouth, the result is a Nasalised Vowel. These
are not found in English but are common in French, the
four varieties being heard in the words *sang, vin, un,* and
son. The vowel heard in *pain, vin,* is simply the vowel
of *père* nasalised. The final syllables -*am*, -*em*, -*um*, etc.
in Latin, elided in poetry before a vowel, were probably
of this nature. If the passage to the Nose is only partially opened, we get the 'nasal twang' of some English
speakers. Nasalised Vowels are generally represented thus,
a^n, o^n, i^n, etc.

The term 'Sonant'² is applied generally to all
'Sonants.' syllable-forming or accent-bearing sounds,
and therefore includes not only Vowels but
certain Consonants when used as syllables. For con-

¹ Broadly speaking; for further distinctions see Sweet, *Primer of Phonetics.*

² The discussion of this term strictly belongs to the chapter on Accent, but is inserted here for convenience.

venience' sake it is often restricted to the latter meaning. The more important of these sounds are the following (the Sonant use of the Consonant being indicated by the diacritic ͅ):

Spirant   (z̧),
Nasals   (b̥) (d̥) (m̥),
Liquids   (l̥) (r̥).

All these except r̥ occur in English, e.g.:

(z̧)   in *As big as Dick* (z̧ big z̧ dik);

(b̥)   in *You c'n gó* (yūw kb̥ gōu̯)[1];

(d̥)   in *London* (lʉndd̥), *Tom an' I* (tom d̥ ʉi̯), *isn't* (izd̥t)[2];

(m̥)   in *Madam* (mædm̥), *Yes'm* (yes m̥), *schism* (sizm̥), *Egham* (egm̥);

(l̥)   in *table* (tei̯bl̥), *When'll you come* (when l̥ yū kʉm).

In the widest sense a Diphthong is the combination
Diphthongs. of two Sonants (or syllable-forming sounds) into one syllable, e.g. (e) and (i) in *day* (dei), (i) and (ə) in *India* (indiə); but the term is generally confined to such combinations as (ei) in *day*, where the first element remains a true Vowel while the second becomes consonantal (Consonant *i* and Consonant *u* are generally written i̯, u̯[3]). With at least 72 possible Vowels and a number of Sonant (i.e. syllable-forming) Consonants, it is obvious that a very great

---

[1] Notice the Uvula-Stop (kb̥) used as a syllable (see above, p. 26).

[2] *Wouldn't, couldn't,* show the Uvula-Stop (dn) used with *t* to form a syllable. In such words as *bacon, token,* three distinct pronunciations may be heard, (bei̯kən) (rather stilted), (bei̯kn) without the Uvula-Stop (most usual), and (bei̯kn̥) with the Uvula-Stop (rather careless). (See above, p. 26.)

[3] Broadly speaking they are the consonants (y) and (w), and except in diphthongs they are so represented in this book, but a distinction must have been made in the original language, at any rate between (i̯) and (y). See Chap. ix.

number of Diphthongs are possible.   The following occur
in English :

(ɐi̯) in *high*,	(au̯) in *how*,	(eə) in *fair*[1],
(ei̯) in *say*,	(ōu̯) in *so*,	(iə) in *here*[1],
(īi̯) in *see*,	(ūw)[2] in *too*,	(ūə) in *poor*[1],
(oi̯) in *boy*.		

In English we also have Triphthongs, e.g. :

Triphthongs.

(ɐi̯ə) in *fire, higher*[1],

(au̯ə) in *hour, power*[1],

(oi̯ə) in *loyal, destroyer*[1].

Of these, *loyal* generally counts as a disyllable, while
fire and *hour*, though generally reckoned as monosyllables,
in poetry can be scanned as disyllables, and vice-versâ
higher and *power* sometimes appear as monosyllables.

It is obvious that, in speaking, the transition from
one sound to another (except where the
Glides.
second is formed in the same Place as the
first, as *nd*) cannot be absolutely instantaneous.   Thus in
pronouncing the word *echo* (ekōu̯) the tongue has to pass
(1) from the *e*-position to the *k*-position, and (2) from the
k-position to the *ō*-position.   Now, as the breath during
these transitions continues to pass through the mouth,
transition-sounds are produced between one position and
the next.   These transition-sounds are known as Glides.
The On-Glide is the transition-sound which precedes a
Vowel or Consonant, the Off-Glide that which
On-Glide.
follows it.   In writing which is swift or care-
Off-Glide.
less, transition-strokes between letters and

---

[1] Final *r* is silent except before a Vowel, e.g. *here* (hiə), but *here and
there* (hiər n̥ ᵭeə).

[2] The second element here is more definitely consonantal, and so is
written *w*, not *u̯*.

words are apt to develop till to a stranger's eye they appear more important than the letters themselves, and thus tend to make the writing illegible. In a similar way, in speech, Glides are capable of developing into ordinary sounds. The importance of Glides in questions of Phonetic Change is therefore obvious. Thus we find the Greek Ἀλκμήνη appears in Plautus as *Alcumena*, δραχμή as *drachuma*, μνᾶ as *mina*. The same principle is seen in such pronunciations as *Henery* for *Henry*, *umberella* for *umbrella*[1]. Similarly we have ἕβδομος for ἕπτ-μος[2], ἀν-δρός for ἀνρός, εἵλκυσα for εἷλκ-σα. The English *thunder* and *timber*, beside their German cognates *Donner* and *Zimmer*, are cases in point.

In the case of an initial vowel (i.e. not of a word but of a breath-group[3]), the sound may have either (1) the 'gradual beginning,' i.e. an On-Glide of the glottis from the breath-position to the voice-position; or (2) the 'clear beginning,' where the breath is kept back till the glottis is ready to produce the sound. In these cases the stress begins on the vowel itself. If, on the other hand, the stress begins *before* the vowel, i.e. on the On-Glide of the 'gradual beginning,' we have the Aspirate, e.g. we have *ho* instead of *o*. Initial *h*, then, in English is the stressed form of the 'gradual beginning.' Between vowels (contrast *hold* with *behold*) the *h* is simply a 'jerk of the breath.'

The Aspirate.

When the Glide between a Stop (*k*, *g*, *t*, *d*, etc.) and the following vowel maintains the stress of the Stop, we have the Aspirated Stops, k^h, g^h, t^h, d^h, etc. The Greek Aspirates χ, θ, φ were of this nature. The same sounds are heard in the Irish pronunciation of English, e.g. *P'hat*, *t'hell*, for *Pat*, *tell*.

Aspirated Stops.

---

[1] Cf. 'Naughty little *Suck-a-Thumb*' for *Suck-Thumb* in the nursery tale.

[2] Through ἔβδ-μος.   [3] See page 36.

CHAPTER III.

ACCENT.

In the previous chapter we have considered the formation and classification of sounds; each sound has been considered separately. We have now to discuss sounds in combination, that is, in words and sentences. It is important to realise at the outset that the division of a sentence into words is a *logical*, not a *phonetic* division; i.e. though in writing (and in thinking) we leave spaces between the words, in speaking there is no spacing at all. The only division made in speaking is the separation into Breath-Groups, i.e. the groups of sounds made between one taking of breath and another. In a long sentence this division usually coincides with the logical division into clauses. It is interesting to note here that in Greek inscriptions and papyri the spacing of words is almost unknown before the Roman period.

Sentence-division.

In discussing the Elements of Language in Chapter I. we spoke of Gesture, Expression of Feature, Speed of Utterance, Tone of Voice, Musical Pitch, and Emphasis or

Stress. The last three concern us here, and we must add another, Quantity or Length.

The Quantity or Length of a sound is its *duration*
Quantity. relative to the adjacent sounds. Phoneticians distinguish five degrees of Quantity;
but three, or even two, are sufficient for practical
purposes[1]. Latin and Greek metre distinguished two.
It is true that difference of Quantity is often accompanied by actual (i.e. organic or structural) difference of
English pro- sound, e.g. in Greek ŏ was narrow and ō wide,
nunciation of while in Latin it was vice-versâ. But we
Latin. must be careful in speaking of Quantity to
clear our minds of such distinctions as are made in the
'old-fashioned' pronunciation prevailing at many English
schools, which distinguishes *mensā* from *mensă* by pronouncing *ā* to rhyme with *hay* (hei), and *quīs* from *quĭs*
by pronouncing *ī* to rhyme with *high* (hɐi̯). A good instance of difference of Quantity (apart from difference of
Stress—see below) is heard in the word *murmur* (which
may be written phonetically məˉmə)[2], the first syllable
taking about twice as long as the second to pronounce.

Loudness or Stress (Emphasis) depends on the *size* of
the vibration-waves of which sound consists.
Stress. It varies with the effort by which the breath
is expelled from the lungs. For practical purposes three
varieties of Stress are sufficient—strong, half-strong, and
weak. These are exemplified in *contradict*, which might be
written CONᴛʀᴀDICT, the third syllable being strong, the

---

[1] In Aryan (see Chapter v.) vowels were probably of three different
lengths.
[2] Strictly speaking there is a slight organic (structural) difference, too.
See table of Vowels, p. 31.

first half-strong, and the second weak. The syllable which
is pronounced with the strongest Stress in a word is said
to bear the Stress-accent. In long words in English two
syllables ordinarily stand out above the others in point of
Stress. Of these one is generally strong, and the other
half-strong. In *impossibility*, for instance, the *-bil-* is
strong and the *im-* half-strong, whereas in the shorter
word *impossible* the *-poss-* alone stands out above the
other syllables. This Stress-accentuation has its parallel
in music, where in bars of more than two or three beats
there is always a secondary accent as well as the primary
accent, i.e. we count **1** 2 3 4, or **1** 2 3 4 5 6.

English metre is a matter of Stress, Greek of Quantity.
Stress and   Though Latin metre by the time of Cicero
Quantity in   had become entirely quantitative, poetry of
Metre.   the earlier period shows traces of Stress-
scansion. Plautus, for instance, in his Iambics and
                    Trochaics, requires an Iambus only at the
Plautus.
                    end of the line, e.g.

Iús iurándum reí seruándae, nón perdéndae cónditúmst;

often neglects elision, e.g.

Mustéla múrem‖abstulit praeter pedes;

and allows scansions such as *pĕr ănnō|nam*; *sĕnĕctú|tem*;
ăge ăbdúc|; and even *quíd íll|aec*. Modern Greek poetry,
                    like English, goes by Stress, as may be seen
Modern   by scanning this line of a modern hexameter
Greek.
                    version of the *Odyssey*:

τόπους δι|ῆλθε, πορ|θήσας τῆς | Τροίας τὴν | ἔνδοξον | πόλιν.

In Elizabethan times attempts were made to write
Quantity in   English poetry according to Latin (quanti-
English   tative) rules of metre. The painful result
metre.   may be gathered from the following hexameter lines from Tottel's *Miscellany* (1557):

Gríslye fa|cés froun|cíng, eke a|gaínst Troy | leáged in | hátred—
Múch lyk on | á moun|táyn thee | trée dry | wýthered | oáken—[1].

A successful attempt in the same direction is Tennyson's
Alcaic Ode to Milton, of which we quote the first stanza:

> O mighty-mouth'd inventor of harmonies,
> O skill'd to sing of Time or Eternity,
> God-gifted organ-voice of England,
> Milton, a name to resound for ages.

But these lines are successful only because they combine
Stress with Quantity throughout.

It is usual to distinguish Pitch from Tone-of-Voice,
Pitch and the one being characteristic of the syllable,
Tone-of-Voice the other of the sentence. To Tone-of-
distinguished. Voice we may assign intonations characteristic of a statement, a question, of indignation, surprise,
pity, endearment, etc. These need no comment. In
Pitch and dealing with Syllable-Intonation or Pitch,
Stress dis- we should first distinguish it clearly from
tinguished. Stress. Stress, as we have seen, depends
on the *size* of the vibrations of which voice consists; Pitch
depends on the *number* (i.e. frequency) of these vibrations.
Pitch, as it were, gives the notes, while Stress adds the
'marks of expression,' loud or soft. From the point of
view of variation of musical tone or Pitch, ordinary
speaking stands midway between the monotone of the
clergyman 'intoning' and actual singing. The monotone
does not vary at all, while, in singing, the musical
'intervals' (e.g. between F and F sharp) are greater as
a rule than in speaking. That is to say, while in music
we use only one note intermediate between A and B,
namely A sharp or B flat, in speaking we use an indefinite
number of intermediate notes, differing from each other by

[1] Quoted by Saintsbury, *Elizabethan Literature*, p. 24.

the smallest fractions of semitones. Pitch-accent, then, indicates musical tone, highness or lowness in the musical scale; and the syllable which has the highest musical tone in a word is said to bear the Pitch-accent.

These two elements of speech, Pitch and Stress, are found in all languages, one or the other generally predominating. In English, Stress predominates. We have many words which (roughly speaking) differ only in Stress, e.g. *cónduct* (noun) and *condúct* (verb), *áttribute* (noun) and *attríbute* (verb). On the other hand, in certain other languages, e.g. Siamese, Pitch is so important an element that to sing a native song to a European air results in sheer nonsense, as many words differ only in Pitch. There are few, if any, examples of English words differing only in Pitch. It is true that the word *rather* used in answer to a question such as *Would you like to go ?* denotes doubtful desire pronounced in one way and intense desire pronounced in another[1]; but this should probably be considered as sentence-intonation or Tone-of-Voice.

In Greek, Pitch almost certainly predominated in Classical times. This is indicated (1) by the accent-system, (2) by phenomena of the language itself, (3) by the statements of native gram-marians. The ancient Greek said but

π α - τ ή ρ,   π ά - τ ε ρ.

The accent-system is ascribed by tradition to the Alexandrian critic, Aristophanes of Byzantium, who is said to have invented the symbols about 200 B.C. with a view to preserving the 'correct' pronunciation. The Acute-accent

_____
[1] A third pronunciation, placing the *Stress*-accent upon the last syllable (*rathér*) is sometimes heard in educated English.

(e.g. τί;) denotes a *rising* tone, as in English *what?*; the Grave-accent denotes either a *falling* or a *level* tone, as in English *look here*, where *look* bears a level tone and *here* a falling tone. Syllables written without accent were understood to be Grave. The Circumflex ('` or ˆ) denotes a *rising-falling* tone, i.e. Acute followed by Grave in the same syllable. This is heard in the English *Oh!* expressing sarcasm, sometimes written *Oho!*[1] Pitch-accent was disregarded in metre in Classical times, but is taken into account in the choliambics of Babrius (170 A.D.), whose last foot always bears the accent on the first syllable. In Modern Greek, Stress predominates, e.g. Αἴγῖνα is now

Stress in Modern Greek.

pronounced Αἴγῖνα with the stress on the first syllable, while in certain dialects Stress has reduced παιδί to π᾽δί, δουλεύω to δ᾽λεύου, ἐγώ to ἰγώ.

In Latin, particularly Early Latin, and probably the vulgar or non-literary Latin of Classical

Accent in Latin.

times, the predominating accentuation was, like the English, Stress. Thus *légimini* was once identical with λεγόμενοι, but, owing to the Stress on the first syllable, the vowels of the other

Vowel-Weakening.

syllables were 'weakened.' Similarly the Stress-accent preserved the *a* in *ágo*, but *súbago* became *subigo*. The same phenomenon is seen in the English *próphet*, which is now indistinguishable from *prófit*; and even Herrick (1648) rhymes *mínute*

Syncope.

with *ín it*. Stress in Early Latin was responsible for the dropping of syllables (Syncope), as in *est*, representing the original *esti*, seen in Greek ἐστί and Sanskrit *asti*. This does not occur in Greek. We may compare *audin* for *audísne*, the

---

[1] This again may be an example rather of sentence-intonation or Tone-of-Voice than of syllable-intonation or Pitch.

forms *dein* and *proin* used before a consonant, *quindecim*
for *quínquedecem*, *uindemia* for *uinidémia* (*demo*), and *ualde*
for *uálide*. In later Latin we find *uirdis* for *uíridis*, whence
comes the French *vert*. English parallels are *búsiness* pronounced (biznis), *régiment* pronounced (redẓmṇt), *chócolate*
pronounced (tṣoklət), *vénison* pronounced (venzṇ), and *don't*
for *dó not*. In America a word like *penitentiary, California*,
often drops *i* before the stressed syllable (penténṣəri, cæl-
fṓnyə). The action of Stress in Low Latin is seen in the
French *âme* for *ánimam*, *même* for *métipsissimum*. We
may compare Cicero's story of the soldiers making the cry
of a fig-seller (*Cauneas*, i.e. 'Caunean figs') into an evil
omen *cáue ne eas*. In the Literary and educated Latin
Accent in   of the Classical period the Stress-accent can
Literary   hardly have been so strong, otherwise Roman
Latin.   poetry must have lost much of its rhythm.
This may be seen by pronouncing a line of Virgil thus:

> Massylíque rúunt équites et odóra cánum uís.

The difference between the Greek and the Latin accent
Effect of   may be seen in Greek loan-words, which ap-
Accent on   pear in Latin with different quantities. Thus
Greek loan-   ἄγκῦρα becomes *ancŏra*, σέλῑνον *selĭnum*, and
words.
                Φίλιππος, the coin, is scanned by Plautus
Philĭppus; while in later times Σοφίᾱ becomes Sofíă,
                ἔρημος *erĕmus*, and εἴδωλον *idŏlum*. In the
Stress in   dialect of Praeneste Stress was even stronger
Praenestine.   than in Early Latin, if we may judge by such
forms as *Mgolnia* for *Magolnia* in inscriptions and *conea*
quoted as Praenestine for *ciconia* ('stork').

We said above that within certain groups there is
                no space between spoken words. A short
Enclitics.
                sentence, then, is phonetically one long word
comprised of syllables of different accent-value. Thus

What did you hit him for? bears a primary accent on

In English.   *hit* and a secondary accent on *What*, just as
impossibility bears a primary accent on *-bil-*
and a secondary accent on *im-*. *Did, you, him, for,* may in
this sentence be termed unaccented words. If, however, we
add the word *then,* we find that *for* at once bears a secondary
accent. This is the principle of Enclitics. Unimportant
words, like unimportant syllables, are unaccented; but, just
as a long word bears a secondary as well as a primary accent,
so, if too many (in English, as a rule, more than two) unimportant words come together, one has to bear an accent.

In Greek.   The accentuation of Enclitics in Greek is
closely parallel, but it should be remembered
that Greek Enclitics were *Pitch*-enclitics, while in English
we have *Stress*-enclitics. In Greek an enclitic not only
'threw its accent back' upon a previous enclitic, but
under certain circumstances changed the accentuation of
a previous accented word, e.g. πατρὸς ὄντος, but πατρός τε.

In Latin.   This has no parallel in English, but in Latin
the principle was recognised in the case of
-que, -ue, and *-ne,* which were spelt as part of the preceding
word. The Romans said *nóctes* but *noctésque,* and Plautus
scans *ín me, intér se,* unless the pronoun is emphatic, with
which we may compare πρός με, κατά σου, in Greek.

CHAPTER IV.

SPELLING AND PRONUNCIATION, WITH A SKETCH OF THE HISTORY OF OUR ALPHABET.

Phonology of Modern Languages—of Dead Languages—*Data for investigating the Pronunciation of Latin and Greek*—Grammarians —Transliterations—Plays on Words—Variations of Ancient Orthography—Changes of Spelling—Pronunciation of Modern Descendants—Cries of Animals in Literature—*Pronunciation of Attic Greek*—Consonants—Vowels—Diphthongs—*Pronunciation of Latin*—Consonants—Vowels—Diphthongs—Greek and Latin Pronunciation contrasted—Greek and English—Latin and English—Double Consonants—Example of Greek Pronunciation—of Latin—*English Spelling*—Causes of the Anomalies— Difficulties of Reform—Example of English Pronunciation— *The Alphabet*—Primitive Beginnings of all Alphabets—Memory-Aids—Message-Sticks—Pictograms— Ideograms — Phonograms —True Alphabet—Egyptian Scripts—the Phoenicians—the Origin of our Alphabet—Oldest Examples—Sister Alphabets— *Earliest Greek Inscriptions* — Alphabet of 750-600 B.C. — Western, Eastern, and Attic Groups—Peisistratus Inscription —Archonship of Eucleides—the 'Breathings'—Eretrian Inscription—Chalcidian Colonies—Rhegine Inscription—Inscription from Volci—*Latin Alphabet*—Appius Claudius—Traces of the Older Alphabet—Greek Letters—Other Modifications— Monumentum Ancyranum—Medieval Orthography—*Subsequent History of our Alphabet* — Cursive — St Patrick — Alcuin — Caroline Minuscule—Black Letter—Roman Type—'Italian' Handwriting.

FROM Chapter II. it will be seen that the number of possible speech-sounds is so large that even if it were possible to represent each by a special sign, the result would be an alphabet too clumsy for practical use. Now though the number of sounds possible to the human voice is very great, the number of sounds which compose any single language is comparatively small[1]. Hence an alphabet of twenty or thirty signs, eked out in some cases by diacritics (accents, diaeresis, etc.), is quite sufficient to express a language for all practical purposes. When, however, we begin to learn a foreign language, we find that many of the letters are used to represent sounds unknown to our own language. In other words, the Sound-Scheme (or Phonology) of English differs widely from that, for instance, of French, though the alphabets are practically identical. Thus, in order to speak and write a foreign language correctly, we must either hear it spoken or study accurate and scientific descriptions of its sounds.

Phonology of Modern Languages.

With dead languages it is a different matter. We have to gather their pronunciation from various data, and when all is done we cannot be quite certain that our results are true.

Of Dead Languages.

The Pronunciation of Latin and Greek has long been a vexed question. We shall not do more here than indicate the data of the problem and the most widely received results.

First, as to the data. These are as follows:

[1] In educated English, without regarding the finer distinctions, about fifty.

(1) Descriptions and discussions of the sounds in the works of writers such as Dionysius of Halicarnassus (*fl.* 30 B.C.) and Varro (*fl.* 70 B.C.).

(2) Transliterations, especially of proper names, from and into other languages, e.g. Κικέρων, *Cyrus*, κῆνσος, σπεκουλάτωρ, *Athenae*, Φαρνάβαζος, Ἰερουσαλήμ, the Welsh *ciwdawd* (Latin *ciuitatem*), the Old English *bisceop* (ἐπίσκοπος through Latin *episcopus*) and *cirice*, our *church* (κυριακόν).

Data for investigating the pronunciation of Latin and Greek.

(3) Plays on words in literature, depending on similarity of sound, e.g. ὦ Βδεῦ δέσποτα for ὦ Ζεῦ, Com. Anon. 338 b, and *Cauneas* for *Caue ne eas*, Cic. *Div.* 2. 40. 84.

(4) The variations of orthography in inscriptions and papyri.

(5) The phonetic changes indicated by well-authenticated change of spelling during the 'lifetime' of the languages.

(6) The actual pronunciation of Modern Greek and the Romance Languages (Italian, Spanish, etc.).

(7) The representation in literature of the cries of animals, e.g. αὖ αὖ the bark of a dog in Ar. *Vesp.* 903, βῆ βῆ the bleat of a sheep in Cratinus Διόν. 5, and the cawing of a crow mistaken for *aue* in Phaedrus *Fab. App.* 2. 22.

We shall now give a scheme of the probable pronunciation of Attic Greek in the 5th and 4th centuries B.C.

Pronunciation of Attic Greek.

(i) CONSONANTS.

    (1) Spirants:

      Breathed—

        σ: as in Eng. *sit*, not as in *rise* (rₑiz).

        σσ: these are probably two spellings of one sound, perhaps like the Eng. *th* (þ) in *thin* doubled[1].

        ττ:

      Voiced—

        σ: before voiced consonants, e.g. σβέννυμι, κόσμος; cf. in Eng. *news* (nyūwz) but *newspaper* (nyūwspeịpə).

        ζ: *zd* as in Eng. *amaz'd* (not *dz* as in Eng. *kids*); cf. 'Αθήναζε for 'Αθηνασ-δε, and διόζοτος found in inscriptions for διόσ-δοτος[1].

    (2) Stops:

      Breathed—

        κ:
        τ: } as in Eng.
        π:

      Voiced—

        γ: (1) as in Eng.; (2) under certain circumstances, e.g. ὀλίγος,— the velar spirant (ꝫ) (Germ. *g* in *Lage*); but this was thought vulgar[2].

        δ:
        β: } as in Eng.

---

[1] Another view is that the pronunciation of σσ or ττ, representing κy-, τy-, was *sh* (ṣ) and of ζ, representing γy-, δy-, *zh* (ẓ); cf. Eng. *nation* (neịṣn̥) but *native* (neịtiv).

[2] In some of the oldest Egyptian Greek papyri ὀλίγος is written ὀλίος.

(3) The Aspirate:

      ': much as in Eng., but considerably weaker, like the second *h* in *hedgehog*.

(4) Aspirated Stops:

    χ: k^h, roughly resembling *kh* in *ink-horn*.

    θ: t^h, roughly resembling *th* in *at-home*.   See page 35.

    φ: p^h, roughly resembling *ph* in *up-hold*.

(5) Nasals:

  Breathed—

    ν:

    μ: probably (1) after Aspirated stops, e.g. ἀριθμός (aritmhos)[1], not (arit^{h}mos); θνήσκω (tnhē̦iskɔ)[1], not (t^{h}nē̦iskɔ); and (2) before the Aspirate, e.g. τὸν ἵππον (tonh ippon).

  Voiced—

    γ: before γ, κ, and χ—as Eng. *ng*, *n*, in *sing*, *sink*.

    ν: (1) initial and medial—as in Eng. (except in words like *sing*, *sink*).

         (2) final—(except before a pause) assimilated in Place to the following consonant, e.g. τὴν πόλιν (tēm polin); ὁ μὲν γέρων (ho meɒ gerɔn) (so found in inscriptions, e.g. ἐγ Κορίνθωι).

    μ: as in Eng.

---

[1] Breathed *m*, *n*, *l*, and *r* are generally spelt phonetically *mh*, *nh*, *lh*, and *rh*.

(6) Liquids :

λ: (1) Breathed after Aspirated Stops, e.g.
        φλοῖσβος (plhoi̯zbos)¹, not (pʰloi̯zbos).
    (2) Voiced elsewhere as in Eng.

ρ: alveolar as in Eng., but trilled as in Low-
    land Scotch.
    (1) Breathed initially and after Aspirated
        Stops and ρ, e.g. ʽΡόδος² (Lat. *Rhodus*);
        χρόνος (krhonos)¹, not (kʰronos); Πύρ-
        ρος (pürrhos), (Lat. *Pyrrhus*).
    (2) Voiced elsewhere as in Eng., e.g. ʼΕρινύς
        (Lat. *Erinys*).

[ξ was *ks* and ψ *ps*, sometimes possibly *gz* and *bz*.]

(ii *a*) VOWELS.

α: short—as in Lowland Scotch *man*.
    long—as in Eng. *father*.
ε: narrow; as in Fr. *été*.
η: as in Fr. *fête*, but wide (not as in Eng. *fate*
    or *feet*).
ι: short—narrow as in Fr. *fini* (not wide as in
    Eng. *pin*).
    long—as in Eng. *see*, but narrow and without
    the final i̯.
o: narrow ; as in Fr. *beau* (not a diphthong as
    in Eng. *so*).
ω: wide (ɔ); somewhat as *o* in Eng. *not*, but
    lengthened (Eng. *aw* (ɔ) is narrow).
υ: (ü) short—as in Fr. *du pain*⎱ (not as in Eng.
    long—as in Fr. *pur*. ⎰ *tune* or *rune*).

---

¹ Breathed *m, n, l,* and *r* are generally spelt phonetically *mh, nh,
lh,* and *rh.*

² In inscriptions the rough breathing (ῤ) is said to occur only once.

(ii *b*)   DIPHTHONGS.

αι: somewhat as in Eng. *line*, but (aι̣) rather than (ɐι̣).

ει: (1) when the result of contraction of ε-ε or 'compensatory lengthening[1],' e.g. φιλεῖτε for φιλέετε, λύειν for λύεεν, τιθείς for τιθέ(ντ)ς, ἔμεινα for ἔμεν(σ)a,—probably as η (see above).

(2) 'true' diphthong, i.e. (eι̣) as λείπω,— much as in Eng. *hay*, but narrow.

οι: somewhat as in Eng. *coin* (see *o*), e.g. τὸ ἱμάτιον became θοἱμάτιον.

υι: this does not occur in Attic inscriptions of the 4th cent. B.C. (e.g. υἱός is written ὑός, Ὠρείθυια Ὠρειθῦα, κατεαγυῖα κατεαγῦα) but has crept into our Classical texts owing to Hellenistic influence. In the 5th cent. the ι must have been pronounced very weakly if at all. In the non-Attic dialects, on the other hand, it persisted, but in them it was a diphthong only in the wider sense (see p. 33), being (ṵi) rather than (uι̣), the *u* consonantal as in Fr. *lui*. Our pronunciation, making *υ* the consonant, is correct only for the non-Attic dialects.

ᾳ:⎫
η:⎬ these were in ancient times generally written
ῳ:⎭ αι, ηι, ωι. In inscriptions and papyri the ι is often omitted altogether; the ι-sound

---

[1] i.e. when a short vowel originally long 'by position' becomes long 'by nature' (or in certain cases diphthongised) on the disappearance of the consonant which originally made it long.

was very weak, and probably had ceased
to be pronounced by the 2nd cent. B.C.
Our present way of writing the ι under-
neath (subscript) came in only about the
12th cent. A.D.

αυ: as in Eng. *cow*.

ευ: somewhat as in Cockney *heaow* for *how*,
i.e. (eṷ) (not as *u* in *use*).

ηυ: original (ēṷ) soon became identical with ευ,
and after the 4th century verbs beginning
with ευ were spelt without the augment.

ου: (1) when the result of contraction or 'compensatory lengthening,' e.g. δηλοῦτε for
δηλόετε, λόγου for λογό(σι)ο, διδούς for
διδό(ντ)ς, βουλή for βολ(ϝ)ή,—a pure (u)-
sound as in Fr. *cou* (not as in Eng. *cow*).

(2) 'true' diphthong, i.e. (oṷ), as in οὐχ,
οὗτος, σπουδή,—much as in Eng. *so*, but
narrow.

ωυ: original (ōṷ) scarcely occurs in Attic (πρωυ-
δᾶν, however, for προαυδᾶν), and soon
became identical with ου; hence the contraction of καὶ οὐ is written κοὐ not κωὐ.

The pronunciation of Latin by educated people
Pronuncia- of the Augustan period was probably as
tion of Latin. follows:

(i) CONSONANTS.

(1) Spirants:

Breathed—

s: as in Eng. *sit* (not as in Eng. *rise*).

f: labiodental as in Eng.; earlier bilabial.

Voiced—

[*s* (z): as in Eng. *rise*; only in the early period between vowels; it soon changed to *r*, e.g. *labōsem* became *labōrem*.]

v[1] (w): weak as in Fr. *ouest*, not so strong as Eng. *w* in *west*.

j[2] (i̯): *y* as in Eng. *yard*.

(2) Stops:

Breathed—

c: as Eng. *k* (never as Eng. *s*).

t: dental as in Fr. and Germ. (not alveolar as in Eng.[3]).

p: as in Eng.

Voiced—

g: as in Eng. *game* (never as in Eng. *gem*).

d: dental (see *t*).

b: as in Eng., but unvoiced before *s* and *t*, e.g. *urbs* (urps), *obtineo* (optineō).

(3) The Aspirate:

h: weaker than initial *h* in Eng.; like the second *h* in *hedgehog*.

(4) Nasals:

n: (1) before *c*, *g*, *q*,—(ŋ) as in Eng. *sink*, *single*.

(2) before other Consonants (except *n*)—nasalised (identical with *m*, see below).

(3) elsewhere as in Eng.

---

[1] Written *u* in the Augustan period and in most modern texts.

[2] Written *i* in the Augustan period and in most modern texts.

[3] See footnote to p. 23.

m: (1) medial and final before most Consonants, and final before Vowels and h[1]—nasalised as in Fr. *empéreur*, except

    i. before m, when it remained unchanged.

    ii. before n, l, and r, when it was assimilated, e.g. *cum nobis* (kun nōbīs), *cum regibus* (kur rēgibus), *tam leuis* (tal lewis).

    iii. before c, g, and q, when it became (ŋ), e.g. *cum quattuor* (kuŋ qwattuor).

  (2) elsewhere as in Eng.

(5) Liquids :

  l: dental (not alveolar as in Eng.).

  r: voiced alveolar as in Eng., but trilled as in Lowland Scotch.

[x was ks; z, th, ph, ch, and rh were used only in Greek words, and had the Greek values, save that the last four were pronounced t, p, c, and r by the uneducated.]

(ii a) VOWELS.

  a: short,—as in Lowland Scotch *man*.
      long,—as in Eng. *father*.

  e: short,—wide, as in Eng. *men*.
      long,—narrow, as in Fr. *fête*.

  i: short,—as in Eng. *pin*.
      long,—as in Eng. *see*, but narrow and without the final $i̯$.

  o: short,—wide, as in Eng. *not*.
      long,—narrow, as in Fr. *beau*.

---

[1] Hence the elision of -*am*, -*em*, etc., in poetry.

u : short,—

> (1) as in Eng. *full*.
>
> (2) in *optimus* or *optumus* and similar words, like Fr. *u* (ü) in *du pain*.

long,—as in Fr. *cou*, Eng. *rune* (not as in Eng. *tune*).

[*y* was used for *v* (ü) in Greek words, e.g. *lyra, gȳrus*, and only appeared in true Latin words[1] in later times, e.g. *sylva, Sylla*.]

(ii *b*) DIPHTHONGS.

> *ae* : first like (aị) (as spelt till 100 B.C.), then it gradually approximated to (ē), becoming identical in the 5th century A.D. (hence in medieval ecclesiastical Latin such forms as *ecclesie* for *ecclesiae*). In the Augustan period *ae* was probably pronounced (æe), i.e. the vowel of *man* followed by that of *men*.
>
> *oe* : first like (oị) (as spelt till 100 B.C.), then it gradually approximated to (ū) as in Fr. *cou*. In the Augustan period it was probably pronounced (öe), i.e. *eu* in Fr. *peu* followed by *e* in Eng. *men*.
>
> *ui* : only a diphthong in the wider sense (see p. 33), being (ụi) rather than (uị); in *huic* and *cui* it was probably pronounced as in Fr. *lui*.
>
> *au* : first like (aụ) (as in Eng. *cow*), then it gradually approximated to narrow *o* (as in Fr. *beau*). Thus *Clodius* was only

---

[1] Except in a few cases of words wrongly thought to be derived from Greek, e.g. *lacryma, inclytus*.

another spelling of *Claudius*. In the Augustan period *au* was probably pronounced (ɔu̯), i.e. *aw* in *law* followed by the *u* in *full*.

eu : (1) the 'true' diphthong disappeared very early, (2) the 'spurious' occurs in contractions such as *neu* for *neue* (newe). It was probably pronounced somewhat as in the Cockney *heaow* for *how*, i.e. (eu̯) (not as *u* in Eng. *use*).

For contrasts between Greek and Latin pronunciation, see :—

Some contrasts.

μ, ν and *m, n,*
ρ and *r,*
ϵ, η and *e,*
o, ω and *o,*
$\upsilon, o\upsilon$ and *u,*
$a\upsilon$ and *au.*

Contrasting Greek with English we should note :—

$\chi, \theta, \phi,$
$\rho,$
$\epsilon, \eta,$
o, ω
$\upsilon, o\upsilon,$

and the diphthongs generally, as well as the absence in Greek of :—

f, v,
w,

and *j* and 'soft' *g* (in *judge*), and *ch* (in *church*).

Contrasting Latin with English we notice :—

c,
t,
v (*u* consonant),
-*an*-, -*en*-, -*am*, -*em*, etc. nasalised,

and the absence of (z) (*s* in *rise*), and of *j* and 'soft' *g* (in *judge*), and *ch* (in *church*).

It should be added that, unlike English, Greek and Latin always pronounced double consonants double, e.g. in λάκκος and *penna* the *k*-sound and the *n*-sound formed part of both syllables, i.e. λάκ-κος, *pen-na*, not λάκ-ος, *pen-a*. English has parallels only in compounds, e.g. *book-case* (bukkeịs), *penknife* (pennụịf), *midday* (middeị).

Double Consonants.

We shall now give extracts from Plato and Cicero, first in the phonetic spelling used to represent sounds throughout this book[1], and then in the ordinary spelling of our texts. It should be remembered, however, that the phonetic spelling is imperfect, and that, particularly in the case of the vowels, the use of the same sign in Greek, Latin, and English, does not necessarily mean that the sounds thus indicated were absolutely identical (see the descriptions of the sounds above).

Examples of Greek and Latin pronunciation.

Extracts from Plato transcribed phonetically.

(i) euthüis oụm m idɔnh o kephalos ēspazdeto te kaị eịpen, ɔ sɔkrates, oụde thamizdēs hēmīɐ katabaịnɔn ēs tom peịraịā: krhēm mentoị. eị meɐ gar egɔ eti en dünameị ēn tū rhāịdiɔs poreụesthaị pros to astü oụden an s edeị deụr ienaị, allh ēmeịs am para se ēịmen: nūn de se krhē püknoteron deụr ienaị: hɔs eụ isth oti emoịge, hosonh aị kata to sɔmh ēdonaị apomaraịnontaị, tosoụton aụksontaị haị peri tūs logūs epithūmiaị te kaị hēdonaị......

Phonetically.

<hr>

[1] Based on the 'Broad Romic Notation' used by Sweet in his *Primer of Phonetics*.

(ii) egɔ d agapɔ, eām mē elaþþɔ[1] katalipɔ toꭐtoịsī, alla brakʰeị ge tini pleịɔ ē parelabon.......

(iii) alla moị eti tosond eịpe : ti megiston oịeị agatʰon apolelaꭐkenaị tū pollēn ūsiāꭐ kektēstʰaị? ho, ē dʰ os, isɔs oꭐk am pollūs peịsaịmi legɔn. eꭐ gar istʰ, epʰē, ɔ sɔkrates, hoti epeịdān tis eꭐgüs ēị tū oịestʰaị teleꭐtēsēn, ēserkhetaị aꭐtɔị deos kaị prhontis peri hɔn emprostʰen oꭐk ēsēịeị.

(i) εὐθὺς οὖν με ἰδὼν ὁ Κέφαλος ἠσπάζετό τε καὶ εἶπεν, Ὦ Σώκρατες, οὐδὲ θαμίζεις ἡμῖν κατα- βαίνων εἰς τὸν Πειραιᾶ· χρῆν μέντοι. εἰ μὲν γὰρ ἐγὼ ἔτι ἐν δυνάμει ἦν τοῦ ῥαδίως πορεύεσθαι πρὸς τὸ ἄστυ, οὐδὲν ἄν σε ἔδει δεῦρο ἰέναι, ἀλλ' ἡμεῖς ἂν παρὰ σὲ ἦμεν· νῦν δέ σε χρὴ πυκνότερον δεῦρο ἰέναι· ὡς εὖ ἴσθι ὅτι ἔμοιγε, ὅσον αἱ κατὰ τὸ σῶμα ἡδοναὶ ἀπομαραίνονται, τοσοῦτον αὔξονται αἱ περὶ τοὺς λόγους ἐπιθυμίαι τε καὶ ἡδοναί.......

In the spell- ing of our texts.

(ii) ἐγὼ δὲ ἀγαπῶ, ἐὰν μὴ ἐλάττω καταλίπω του- τοισί, ἀλλὰ βραχεῖ γέ τινι πλείω ἢ παρέλαβον.......

(iii) ἀλλά μοι ἔτι τοσόνδε εἰπέ· τί μέγιστον οἴει ἀγαθὸν ἀπολελαυκέναι τοῦ πολλὴν οὐσίαν κεκτῆσθαι; Ὅ, ἦ δ' ὅς, ἴσως οὐκ ἂν πολλοὺς πείσαιμι λέγων. εὖ γὰρ ἴσθι, ἔφη, ὦ Σώκρατες, ὅτι, ἐπειδάν τις ἐγγὺς ᾖ τοῦ οἴεσθαι τελευτήσειν, εἰσέρχεται αὐτῷ δέος καὶ φροντὶς περὶ ὧν ἔμπροσθεν οὐκ εἰσῄει.

PLATO, *Rep.* I. 328 C, 330 B, 330 D.

In reading the following phonetic transcription of an extract from Cicero it should be understood that the 'intrinsic' length of vowels long 'by position' cannot be completely determined, though in some cases, e.g. a vowel before *ns* or *nf*, the statements of the ancient authorities are explicit.

---

[1] *Or* elasɔ (see p. 47).

Extract from Cicero transcribed phonetically.

Phonetically.

qwod prekātus ā dīs immortālibus suᴺ, yūdikēs, mōr īᴺstitūtōqwe māyōruᴺ illō diē qw auspikātō komitiīs keᴺturiātīs lūkium mūrēnaᴺ kōᴺ- suler renuᴺtiāwī, ut ea rēs mī, fidēī magistrātuīqwe meō, populō plēbīqwe rōmānææ ben atqwe fēlīkiter ēwēnīret, ideᴺ prekor ab īsdeᴺ dīs immortālibus ob ēyusdeᴺ homi- nis kōᴺsulātuᴺ ūnā kuᴺ salūt optineᴺduᴺ, et ut westrææ meᴺtēs atqwe seᴺteᴺtiææ kuᴺ populī rōmānī woluᴺtātibus suffrāgiīsqwe kōᴺseᴺtiaᴺt eaqwe rēs wōbīs populōqwe rō- mānō pākeᴺ trāᴺqwillitāteᴺ ōtiuᴺ kōᴺkordiaᴺqwe afferat …qwææ kuᴺ ita siᴺt, yūdikēs, et kuᴺ omnis deōruᴺ im- mortāliuᴺ potestās aut trāᴺslāta sit ad wōs aut kerte kommūnikāta wōbīskuᴺ, īdeᴺ kōᴺsuleᴺ westrææ fidēī kommeᴺdat, qwī aᴺteā dīs immortālibus kommeᴺdāwit, ut ēyusdeᴺ hominis wōke et dēklārātus kōᴺsul et dēfēᴺsus benefikiuᴺ populī rōmānī kuᴺ westr atqw omniuᴺ kīwiuᴺ salūte tueātur…….

In the spell- ing of our texts.

Quod precatus a dis immortalibus sum, iudices, more institutoque maiorum illo die, quo auspicato comitiis centuriatis L. Murenam consulem renuntiaui, ut ea res mihi, fidei magistratui- que meo, populo plebique Romanae bene atque feliciter eueniret, idem precor ab isdem dis immortalibus ob eius- dem hominis consulatum una cum salute obtinendum, et ut uestrae mentes atque sententiae cum populi Romani uoluntatibus suffragiisque consentiant eaque res uobis populoque Romano pacem, tranquillitatem, otium, con- cordiamque adferat…quae cum ita sint, iudices, et cum omnis deorum immortalium potestas aut translata sit ad uos aut certe communicata uobiscum, idem consulem uestrae fidei commendat, qui antea dis immortalibus com-

mendauit, ut eiusdem hominis uoce et declaratus consul
et defensus beneficium populi Romani cum uestra atque
omnium ciuium salute tueatur.

CICERO, *pro Mur.* I. 1, 2.

In dealing with Greek and Latin we take the written
English language first, and from it deduce the pro-
spelling. nunciation; in the case of our own language
we take the actual sounds first, and think of the written
language as merely representing those sounds. On comparing the English signs with the sounds they represent,
Identical we are at once struck by the enormous
sounds vari- number of anomalies. For instance, we
ously spelt. represent the sounds

(aṵ) by *ou* (*out*), *ough* (*plough*), *ow* (*how*);

(ɐḭ) by *i* (*line*), *eigh* (*height*), *igh* (*high*), *y* (*by*),
ye (*rye*);

(eḭ) by *a* (*rate*), *ai* (*rail*), *ay* (*hay*), *eigh* (*weigh*),
ey (*whey*);

(k) by *k* (*kill*), *c* (*cat*), *ck* (*stick*), *ch* (*stomach*), *que*
(*barque*);

(ṋ) by *en* (*token*), *on* (*person*), *and* (*bread-and-
butter*).

Similarly, identical spellings are variously pronounced, e.g.

Identical *use* (noun) and *use* (verb),
spellings *freight* and *sleight*,
variously *vase* and *case*,
pronounced. *room* and *wood*,
war and *tar*.

Such anomalies doubtless occur in every alphabet, and
are due to various causes. The chief cause
Causes of is that language is always changing natu-
anomalies. rally, while an alphabet can only be changed
artificially. Hence, in order to represent the sounds of a

language accurately, the signs have to be reformed from time to time. Where the knowledge of letters is confined to a comparatively small part of a community, such reforms are easily made by agreement among the users of them. Where however, as in our own case, by far the larger number of the speakers of the language can read and write, any wide reform, even if it could be agreed to among the learned, would lead to great confusion among the half-educated masses. Another difficulty in the way of revising the spelling of a language spoken over a wide area, would be local varieties of pronunciation. A simple word like *warm* is pronounced differently in the West of England, the Midlands, and the North. If the new spelling had to satisfy the phonetic needs of America and Australia, the difficulty from this cause would be still greater. Small reforms will doubtless be introduced from time to time, such as the dropping of superfluous letters, e.g. in *develope, programme*, but it is extremely unlikely that any drastic reform of English spelling will take place under the present conditions.

Difficulties of reforming spelling.

We give a specimen of English in the phonetic spelling used above.

Extract from O. W. Holmes transcribed phonetically.

wel—ɐi̯ kānt bi sævidẓ wiđ yū fə wontiɐ tə lāf[1], ṇd ɐi̯ lɐi̯k tə mei̯k yū lāf, wel ənɐf, when[2] ɐi̯ kæn. bət đen əbzōv đis: if đə sens əv đə ridikyələs iz wɐn sɐi̯d əv ṇ impresəbḷ nei̯tsə, its veri wel; bət if đæts ɔl đeər[3] iz in ə mæn, hīi̯d betər əv bīi̯n[4] ṇ ei̯p ət wɐns, ṇd sōu̯ əv stud ət đə hed əv iz prəfesṇ. lāfter ṇ tiəz ə ment tə tēn đə

---

[1] N. educated Eng. 'læf.'

[2] S. educated Eng. often 'wen.'

[3] Or (with less stress) 'đər.'   [4] Or 'bin.'

whiịlz[1] əv ðə seịm məsịịnəri əv sensəbiləti[2]; wɐnz wind-
paụər ṇ ði ɐðə wɔtə-paụə : ðæts ɔl.   aịv ɔfṇ hɐd ðə prəfesə
tɔk əbaụt histeriks z̦ bīịɐ neịtsəz klevərist iləstreịsṇ əv ðə
rəsiprəkḷ kṇvētəbiləti[2] əv ðə tūw steịts əv whits[1] ðīịz ækts
ə ðə mænifesteịsṇz ; bət yūw[3] məị sīị it evri deị in tsịildrṇ ;
ṇd if yū wont tə tsōụk wið stɐịfḷd tiəz ət sɐịt əv ðə
trænsiz̦ṇ[4], z̦ it sōụz itself in ōụldə yiəz, gōụ ṇ sīị mistə
bleịk pleị dz̦esi rɔrḷ.

The passage stands thus in the ordinary spelling :

'Well—I can't be savage with you for wanting to
laugh, and I like to make you laugh, well enough, when I
can.   But then observe this : if the sense of the ridiculous
is one side of an impressible nature, it is very well; but
if that is all there is in a man, he had better have been an
ape at once, and so have stood at the head of his profession.   Laughter and tears are meant to turn the wheels
of the same machinery of sensibility; one is wind-power
and the other water-power: that is all.   I have often
heard the Professor talk about hysterics as being Nature's
cleverest illustration of the reciprocal convertibility of the
two states of which these acts are the manifestations; but
you may see it every day in children; and if you want to
choke with stifled tears at sight of the transition, as it
shows itself in older years, go and see Mr Blake play
Jesse Rural.'

O. W. HOLMES, *The Autocrat of the Breakfast Table*, IV.

The remainder of the Chapter will be devoted to a
sketch of the History of our Alphabet.

---

[1] S. educated Eng. often ' wiịlz,' ' witṣ.'
[2] Or ' sensibiləti,' ' kṇvētibiləti.'
[3] This word varies between ' yū ' and ' yūw ' according to the stress.
[4] S. educated Eng. often ' trānsizn.'

Just as it used to be thought that language was put into man's mouth ready-made by the Creator, so the Alphabet was believed to have been the deliberate invention of a single man. It is now known that it has been evolved from just as primitive beginnings as speech.

History of our Alphabet.

Nearly all savages use some system of Memory-Aids, i.e. some tangible object is kept as a record, or sent as a message. Herodotus (iv. 98) tells us how when Darius crossed the Danube to invade Scythia, he gave to the Ionians whom he left to guard his bridge of boats a thong in which he had tied sixty knots. They were to untie a knot each day, and if when they were all untied he had not returned they were to sail away to their own lands[1]. Among the ancient Peruvians the knotted-thong system of aiding the memory was elaborately developed. Their *quipu* was a system of strings, consisting of a main cord, to which were attached at given distances thinner cords of different colours, each knotted in a particular way. Red strings stood for soldiers, yellow for gold, white for silver, and so on, while a single knot meant ten, a double knot a hundred, etc. A similar system is still in use in Peru for registering cattle. Comparatively recently, sums of money lent to the British Government were recorded on Tally-sticks, i.e. notched sticks split down the middle, of which one half was kept in the Exchequer and the other by the lender of the money. The word *indenture*, meaning a kind of agreement, is due to a similar custom, duplicate deeds being cut with notched edges to fit one another. The custom of dividing a bone

Memory-Aids.

Tally-sticks.

---

[1] The familiar ' knot in the handkerchief' is a modern parallel.

or coin between two parties to a covenant was well known in Greece and Rome. Cf. Hdt. vi. 86, Eur. *Med.* 613, and the following from the Comic Fragments:

σύμβολα and *tesserae.*

διαπεπρισμένα

ἡμίσε' ἀκριβῶς ὡσπερεὶ τὰ σύμβολα.

(Eubul. Ξοῦθ. 1.)

The Latin equivalent for σύμβολον was *tessera*, which was used for the tablet employed for making known the watchword to the Roman troops, as well as in the narrower sense of a tally, or token of covenant, particularly between friends and their descendants. Cf. Liv. 7. 35. 1, and the following from Plautus:

A. Ego sum ipsus quem tu quaeris...
B. Si ita est, tesseram conferre si uis hospitalem.

(*Poen.* 5. 2. 87.)

Robinson Crusoe uses the primitive type of Almanac when he cuts small notches for weekdays and large ones for Sundays.

For examples of the Message-stick it is not necessary to go to the savages of Australia or Africa. The Spartan σκυτάλη was doubtless a development of this. The 'fiery-cross,' once used for gathering the Highland clans, is well-known. In the Old Testament (1 Sam. xi. 7) Saul slaughters a yoke of oxen and sends round pieces of them to serve the same purpose. In the Middle Ages it was customary to send a signet-ring with the bearer of an important message, as a token of his *bona fides*.

Message-sticks.

The next step in the development of the Alphabet was the Pictorial stage, in which a picture of a thing is given, to express the thing first actually and then metaphorically. This system is seen

Pictograms.

combined with the last on the grave-posts of Red Indians. For instance, so many strokes on the right of the dead man's totem (e.g. a tortoise, or a crane, the sign of his clan) indicate the number of big battles in which he fought, so many marks on the left the number of treaties of peace to which he was a party; a pipe denotes peace, and a hatchet war. Treaties between the United States and the Indians and between Great Britain and the Maoris, dating from the middle of the nineteenth century, are drawn up in similar style. A sur-
Civilised survivals. vival of the Pictogram is the modern map, especially those of a century or two ago, where instead of a round spot a picture of buildings is given to represent a town. We may compare the crossed swords used to denote the site of a battle, the signboards of old inns, the signs for the pieces in newspaper chess-problems, the planet-signs in almanacs, and the symbol + used for Charing Cross, King's Cross, etc.

Shading insensibly into the Pictographic stage is that
Ideograms. of Ideograms. From the picture representing a thing either actually or by an easily intel- ligible metaphor, writing advanced to denoting things by mere emblems or symbols whose connexion with the things denoted is a matter of teaching or experience. Such symbols in use with us are & denoting 'and,' + to show addition, − subtraction, = 'equals.' Ideo-
Aztec writing. grams are found in the remains of the Aztec writings of Mexico, combined with the more obvious pictogram. Thus a piece of bread protruding from a mouth denotes eating; the symbol for water, placed between the lips, denotes drinking; the ex- tended arms, a negation ; while the names of persons and

places are represented by symbolic figures, e.g. 'Grasshopper Hill' by a hill and a grasshopper. In the same writings a nearer approach to the Phonetic stage is seen, namely the

The Rebus.

picture-pun or *rebus*, which is still used among ourselves as a puzzle or guessing-game, e.g. an eye, a saw, a boy, a swallow, a goose, a berry, standing for the sentence 'I saw a boy swallow a gooseberry'[1].

The Phonetic stage is reached when a certain symbol

Phonograms.

is used to denote a certain sound-group *whatever its meaning*. The earlier forms of the Chinese alphabet (the language is Monosyllabic) contain examples of all the above stages. Thus 'sun' is a circle, 'moon' a crescent (Pictograms); 'strife' two women, 'hermit' a man and a mountain (Ideograms);

Early Chinese examples.

while *chow* means among other things 'ship,' so that a picture of a ship stands for the sound-group *chow* under all circumstances (Phonogram), modifiers or key-signs being added to show which *chow* is meant, e.g. a ship plus the sign for 'water' means 'ripple,' plus the sign for 'speech' means 'loquacity[2].'

European languages are Polysyllabic. Hence the

True Alphabet.

Alphabet as we know it in Europe has gone a step farther. In the Alphabetic stage, not each sound-group, but (roughly speaking) each *sound*, whether vowel or consonant, has its particular symbol.

Though the theory that our Alphabet is derived from

Egyptian scripts.

the Egyptian writing is no longer held, we shall now give some account—as illustrating the development of all alphabets—of the

---

[1] Clodd, *Story of the Alphabet*.

[2] In later Chinese writing the picture-letters have been so far modified as to be generally unrecognisable as such.

Hieroglyphics. The Egyptians used *some* true alphabet-signs as early as 5000 years B.C., but never attained to an entire system of them. The majority of the signs of their script remained pictorial. Egyptian writing is of three kinds, Hieroglyphic, Hieratic, and Demotic. Demotic was a modification of Hieratic, and Hieratic of Hieroglyphic.

(1) The Hieroglyphs (1700 in number) contain picto-grams, ideograms, and phonograms, and date from at least 4777 B.C., which is the year assigned by Professor Flinders Petrie to the foundation of the First Dynasty by Menes. The Hieroglyphs were too clumsy for writing purposes and became practically restricted to monuments.

(2) The Hieratic characters were an abridged form, better suited to the pen or brush of reed used by the priests for writing on the papyrus. In fact, they formed a *cursive* script. The earliest papyrus we possess dates from about 3600 B.C.

(3) The Demotic characters came into use much later, about 900 B.C. They are a still simpler form of the Hieroglyphic, used, as their name implies, by the people as opposed to the priests, i.e. they were the ordinary writing of daily life.

In the time of the Ptolemies (320–40 B.C.) it was customary to make known matters of public importance in Hieroglyphic, Demotic, and Greek. This is the case with the famous Rosetta Stone. This slab, now in the British Museum, proved the key to the interpretation of the Egyptian writing.

Rosetta Stone.

Antiquity is almost unanimous in ascribing the intro-duction of the Alphabet into Greece to the Phoenicians. A comparison of the Greek names of the letters ἄλφα, βῆτα, etc., with

The Phoenicians.

the Hebrew names (given in the Bible version of the
119th Psalm) shows at once the connexion between the
Greek and Semitic scripts. Now in Hebrew the names of
the letters have a meaning, in Greek they have none.
Aleph means 'ox,' *Beth* 'house,' *Gimel* 'camel,' and so on.
This is only one of the facts which, combined with the
ancient testimony, would seem to justify us in assuming
that the Greek Alphabet came from the Phoenicians.
Assuming for the moment that this was so, the next

*Their con-
nexion with
Egypt.* question is, whence did the Phoenicians get
it? Classical tradition points to Egypt. We
know that the Phoenicians were the great
traders of the Mediterranean world from the time of Hiram
and Solomon (1030 B.C.) to the time of Hannibal and the
Scipios. To a nation of trading instincts a workable alphabet is almost a necessity, and the connexion of the
Phoenicians with Egypt is undoubted. From 1600 to
1300 B.C. their country was a dependency of the
Pharaohs, and in 1250 B.C. there was a Tyrian quarter
of Memphis.

Till recent years the view was widely held that the
Greek Alphabet came from the Phoenician,

*The origin of
our Alphabet.* and the Phoenician from the Hieratic. Discoveries in the Aegean, however, and especially
in Crete, carrying the Mycenean or Aegean culture back
to the third millennium B.C., have made it necessary to
revise this theory. Professor Flinders Petrie now declares
the history of the Alphabet to be as old as civilisation.

*Mediter-
ranean
signary.* According to him a great signary or sign-
system (not a true Alphabet[1]) was in use all
over the Mediterranean in 5000 B.C. This

---

[1] The different forms of the symbols can be counted by hundreds.

system was developed variously in different countries. It was contemporary with the Hittite writings and the Egyptian Hieroglyphs. For many centuries it remained in the pre-alphabetic stage, a system of signs with more or less recognised meanings in different localities, but no more. The change of attributing a letter-value to each sign was probably the outcome of Phoenician commerce. When the Dorian Migrations (1100 B.C.?) swept away the Mycenean civilisation, the Phoenicians quickly seized the opportunity of extending their trade throughout Greece, and established depôts in the ports of the Aegean. Thus those particular versions of the great Mediterranean sign-system which had been current in Greece in Mycenean times became, as it were, condensed, simplified, and unified by the needs of commerce.

Simplified by trade.

Just as the successive invasions of England by peoples speaking a foreign language have cleared our language of superfluous inflexions and awkward ambiguities, so the trade fostered by the Phoenicians, by bringing together users of different varieties of the Mediterranean system, tended to clear the system of superfluous signs and of symbols which were peculiar in form or value to any one district. It is probable that the Phoenicians used the Mediterranean signs at first for numerals and trade-marks. The Greek Alphabet of later times, as is well known, was employed as a numeral-system, and in the time of Aristophanes Corinthian horses were branded with a Koppa, ϙ, the initial letter of Κόρινθος in the alphabet employed at Corinth in early times. Anyhow, the old sign-system of a hundred or more symbols, under the unifying influence of trade became an Alphabet of twenty-two or twenty-three letters, varying, it is true, in

Use as Numerals and Trade-marks.

shape and value according to the locality, but each representing a single sound.

The oldest examples of this Alphabet are the inscriptions
on fragments of a bronze bowl discovered in

Baal Lebanon.

Cyprus, which bears an inscription dedicating
it to Baal Lebanon, dating from before 1000 B.C., and the
famous Moabite Stone, set up about 890 B.C.

Moabite
Stone.

by Mesha king of Moab to commemorate his
rebellion against Israel.

The Greek Alphabet was not the only script which
sprang from this source. Hebrew, Syriac,

Other Alpha-
bets of the
same origin.

Arabic, the Indian languages, Bengali,
Gujarati, Tamil, etc., as well as those of
Burma, Ceylon, Korea, and Siam—these are only a few
of the languages which owe their alphabets, if not to
the Phoenicians, at any rate to the great Mediterranean
sign-system which the Phoenicians adopted and system-
atised.

As the trading Alphabet spread throughout Greece
and became adopted for general purposes of record and
communication, the Greeks found that some of the letters
were not wanted in their language, while some of their
native sounds were unrepresented. Thus we

*Earliest
Greek
inscriptions.*

find in the earliest extant Greek inscriptions
excavated at Athens and Corinth and in the
island of Thera (750 ?—600 B.C.) that the superfluous con-
sonant-symbols 'aleph,' 'he,' 'yod,' and 'ayin'—to give
them their Hebrew names—are used for the vowels
a, e, i, and *o,* which were not written in Phoenician and
Hebrew. Ϝ, Digamma or Vau (i.e. conso-

Ϝ

nantal *u,* pronounced *w*), which is necessary
to the scansion of the Homeric poems (9th century B.C.?),
was still required, as is shown by the invention of a new

symbol for its vowel-equivalent *u*, namely Y or V. The

Y
original order of the letters remained the same, and upsilon was placed at the end. The earliest Greek inscription (found at Athens) also

X
contains X with the value χ. This was probably adopted from the non-Hellenic Carian alphabet, in which it has the value *h*. But in most of the extant inscriptions dating from before 600 B.C. the Palatal Aspirate is represented by ⱐH (*κh*) and the Labial Aspirate by ⌐H (*πh*), while though ‡ (*ξ*) represents *κσ*, a separate symbol is not thought necessary for

Alphabet of
750—600 B.C.
πσ or *πhσ*. The following, *allowing for many local variations in shape and position*, may be taken as a rough representation of the Greek Alphabet down to about 600 B.C.:

Λ ᗺ ⅂ Δ ϟ Ⅎ ⵣ ⊟ ⊕ ⟨ ⵏ ⌐ ᙏ Ⅿ ‡ ο ⌐ Ⲙ Φ ϙ ⵠ Τ Υ [X],

with the values

a β γ δ ε-η ϝ ζ(h) θ ι κ λ μ ν ξ o-ω π ⵠ (q) ρ σ τ υ [χ].

It should be noticed that—

one symbol does duty for ε and η,

one symbol does duty for ο and ω,

ϝ, digamma (*w*) is still in use,

Ⴖ, which in the form H was afterwards used for η, is here used for the rough breathing,

after π we have ⵠ (or M, as it appears in some inscriptions), probably corresponding to the Hebrew 'shin' or *sh* (ṣ); this letter survived as a numeral, 900;

ϙ, koppa (*q*), is still used for *κ* before ο and υ,

φ and ψ, and, generally speaking, χ, are absent,

these early inscriptions are *retrograde*, i.e. written from right to left (cf. the forms of *β*, *ε*, above); before our left-to-right system prevailed people also wrote

βουστροφηδόν ('winding as one ploughs with oxen'),
i.e. opposite ways in alternate lines. In this style were
written the laws of Solon (594 B.C.) and some of the
Abu-Simbel inscriptions (590)[1]. Hebrew is still written
from right to left, while Chinese goes vertically.

After about 600 B.C. the sign X becomes general, and
the new symbols Φ and Ψ (probably adopted like X from
the Carian alphabet) begin to occur.

The local variations found existing at this epoch are
Western, generally arranged in three groups, Western
Eastern, and and Eastern, and an intermediate group to
Attic Groups. which Attic belongs. The distinction lies in
the different values and order of Ξ, X, Φ, and Ψ.

WESTERN	ATTIC	EASTERN
Comprising most of Greece Proper and the Western Colonies	Comprising Attica, Aegina, and the Northern states of the Peloponnese	Comprising the Aegean and the cities of Asia Minor
	XΣ = ξ	
Ξ in the form ⊞[2]	[Ξ not used]	Ξ = ξ
X (or +) = ξ	X = χ	X = χ
Φ = φ	Φ = φ	Φ = φ
ΦΣ = ψ	ΦΣ = ψ	
Ψ = χ	[Ψ not used in Attica and Aegina]	Ψ = ψ
order X, Φ, Ψ	order Φ, X	order Φ, X, Ψ

[1] See below.
[2] Only as a superfluous letter.

It will be noticed that the value of φ is the same throughout, and that the Attic Group approximates to the Eastern.

The Western Group will be discussed later in connexion with the Italic Alphabets which are descended from it.

Of the Eastern Group (called also the Ionic Alphabet) the most important documents after the early examples from Thera mentioned above, are the famous inscriptions of Abu-Simbel. These were carved by Greek mercenaries of the Egyptian king Psammetichus II. (594—589 B.C.) on the legs of two colossal figures which are seated before the temple of Abu-Simbel in Nubia. The longest of these inscriptions is shown upon the opposite page, and may be transcribed as follows:

Eastern.
Abu-Simbel.

βασιλεος ελθοντος ες Ελεφαντιναν Ψαματιχο

ταυτα εγραψαν τοι συν Ψαμματιχοι τοι Θεοκλος

επλεον· ηλθον δε Κερκιος κατυπερθε 'υις ο ποταμος

ανιη αλογλοσος δ ηχε Ποτασιμτο Αιγυπτιος δε Αμασις

εγραφε δ αμε Αρχον Αμοιβιχο και Πελεῖος Ουδαμο

As usual in Greek inscriptions prior to the Roman period, the words are not spaced. Comparing this inscription with the older Alphabet given above, we may notice—

the absence of Ϝ in βασιλε[Ϝ]ος,

the use of Ͱ for η[1], and a dash (') for the rough breathing in 'υις,

the use of φ and ψ.

Comparing later Greek we see—

---

[1] This use of Ͱ or ⊢ was probably suggested by the name of the letter, which by the loss of the aspirate (now ceasing to be pronounced in Ionic) passed from Heta to Eta.

the use of ο for ου and ω (Ψαματιχο[υ], Θεοκλο[υ]s,
and αλογλοσος for αλλογλωσσους),
the use of single for double consonants doubtful
(Ψαμματιχοι and Ψαματιχο, and αλογλοσος),
the use of ϙ for κ before ο (Πελεϙος).
Notice also the ι written beside ō; our habit of writing
ῳ, ᾳ, etc., dates only from the 12th century A.D. In
translating, stops should be put at επλεον and at ανιη.
The first τοι = οἱ (as in Herodotus), the second τοι = τῷ.
'υις (υῖς) is Doric for οἷ 'whither'—'as far as the river
allowed them,' i.e. to the Second Cataract. The αλογλοσος
(ἀλλογλώσσους) are the Greek mercenaries. The last line
stands for ἔγραφε δ' ἀμὲ ῎Αρχων ᾿Αμοιβίχου (ὁ ᾿Αμ.) καὶ
Πέλεκος Οὐδάμου (ὁ Εὐδάμου), 'Archon son of Amoebichos
and Pelekos son of Eudamos wrote our names.' ἀμὲ is
Doric for ἡμᾶς.

In another of the inscriptions, which consists simply of
a proper name, ᾿Αγήσερμος, the rough breathing is indicated by ⊟ (i.e. H) and η by ε. This compared with υῖς,
ἦλθον, etc. above shows the transition of the symbol H
from η to the rough breathing.

Among Attic inscriptions we may notice the elegiac
couplet mentioned by Thucydides, vi. 54,
Attic.
found in 1877. Its date is about 515 B.C.
Peisistratus.
It runs as follows:

Μνεμα τοδε hες αρχες Πεισιστ[ρατος Ηιππιο]¹
υιος θεκεν Απολλονος Πυ[θιο]¹ εν τεμενε.

In comparing with the Abu-Simbel inscriptions we may notice—

ε for η, and H for the rough breathing (indicated above by h),

ει and ε indiscriminately for later ει (Πεισιστρατος, τεμενε).

We again have ο for ω (Απολλονος).

Previous to 403 B.C. the Attic Alphabet used ΧΣ for ξ and ΦΣ for ψ; E stood for ε, η, or ει, and O for ο, ω, or ου. Thus Thucydides wrote ΒΟΛΕ for βολή, βουλή, or βούλει, and ΕΛΘΟΜΕΝ for ἤλθομεν or

Archonship of Eucleides.

ἔλθωμεν. In that year, the archonship of Eucleides, a great change was effected in Attic writing. This was the adoption of the Eastern or Ionic Alphabet as the official² Athenian script. The

Ω, H

reform was due to Archinus. From early times certain users of the Eastern Alphabet had distinguished ŏ from ō by using Ω (an open or wide O) for one or the other. In the Abu-Simbel inscriptions we noticed H used by one man for η and by another for h. By the time Archinus introduced the Eastern Alphabet from Samos, Ω had been definitely

h

assigned to ō and H to η. The Athenians had hitherto used H for h; but for the last hundred years at least, the sound h had been weak and its representation in inscriptions uncertain and irregular. It now ceased to be represented in the Athenian Alphabet.

---

¹ The letters within brackets are restored.
² It had been used in private documents for some time before.

The 'Rough Breathing,' originally ⊢, then ∟, though it
appears to have been known in some form to
Aristotle, was generally ascribed along with
the accent-system to Aristophanes of Byzan-
tium. It occurs but rarely in the older papyri (300–1 B.C.).
The 'Smooth Breathing' is never found either in inscriptions or in papyri, and does not occur regularly till the
MSS. of the 7th century A.D. It was never more than a
negative sign, used to emphasise the absence of the
aspiration. The two Breathings assumed their present
form about 1000 A.D.

The
'Breathings.'

The peculiarities of the Alphabets of the Western
Group are, as we have seen, as follows:

Western
Group.

⊧ in the form ⊞, but as a superfluous letter,

X = ξ,

φ𝈿 = ψ,

Ѵ = χ.

Order of the last three letters—X, φ, Ѵ.

In this group the chief interest lies in inscriptions
from Chalcis and Eretria in Euboea and
their colonies in the west. The following
Eretrian inscription, dating from about
470 B.C., has been found on a statue-base at Olympia:

Chalcis and
Eretria.

ΦΙΛΕΣΙΟΣΕΠΟΙΕ   Φιλήσιος ἐποίει.

ERETRIEΣTOIΔΙ   Ἐρετριεῖς τῷ Δί.

Here we may notice, as in the Ionic and Attic inscriptions,
E for ε, η, and ει, and TOI for τῷ. The chief point
is the shape of π and ρ. A slight curve to the short
upright in Π (as is found in contemporary inscriptions)
would foreshadow the Latin P (p), and ρ has already the
beginning of the 'tail' which turned P into R. There is

a Latin inscription extant which in point of the development of these two symbols is actually *less* advanced than
this. In the inscription found in the Comitium in 1899
(ascribed to the 5th century) P and Π have the values *r*
and *p* respectively (see footnote on p. 104).

In the 8th and 7th centuries Chalcis sent out colonists

Chalcidian
Colonies.
to Italy and Sicily, and founded Cumae,
Neapolis, Rhegium, Leontini, Himera, and
other cities. It is probable that the Italic
Alphabets, including the Latin, were derived from those
in use at one or more of these towns.

A Rhegine inscription of the middle of the 5th
century contains the following words:
ΗΟ𐌘 (ὡς); VREMATON (χρημάτων); EV+AMEN (εὐξά-
μην). Note here—

  V for χ,
  + (χ) for ξ,
  H (h),
  V (v),

and the shape of ρ.

The following inscriptions from Volci in Italy also
show the development of the Latin letters:

  (i) 𐌘ΟϘVΛVϽ (retrograde): Γλαῦκος (c. 500 B.C.)
Notice—

  Ϙ (koppa) Latin Q,
  V   Latin L,
  Ͻ   Latin C.

  (ii) ΙΕVS: Ζεύς (c. 450 B.C.).

Notice the shapes of ζ, v, and ς, the last being identical
with the Latin S.

Thus when the Latins came to require an alphabet

for purposes of trade, they found the inhabitants of the
neighbouring Greek cities, such as Cumae
*Latin
Alphabet.*   and Naples, in possession of some such
Alphabet as this:

A B C (⟨) Δ E F Z H ⊕ I Κ L M N O Γ Ϙ R S (ξ) T V X ⊕ Ψ,

with the values

$a \; b \quad c \quad d \; e \; \mathrm{F} \; \zeta \; h \; \theta \; i k \; l \; m \; n \; o \; p \; q \; r \quad s \quad t \; u \; x \; \phi \; \chi.$

The aspirates θ (t^h as in *at-home*), ϕ (p^h as in *uphold*),
Superfluous   and χ (k^h as in *ink-horn*), expressed sounds
signs as   unknown to Latin, and the signs $\oplus$, $\oplus$, Ψ,
Numerals.   were accordingly dropped from the alphabet
proper, though from $\oplus$ or its variant $\odot$ came the numeral
C = 100 (*centum*), from $\oplus$ came the M = 1000 (*mille*),
while **D**, the half of $\oplus$, became the sign for 500; Ψ came
to be written ⊥ and finally L, indicating 50.

The early Latins seem to have failed to distinguish
the sound *k* from the sound *g* ('hard'). In early inscriptions C or ⟨ is used for either, while K
C, K.   gradually disappears; e.g. VIRCO for *uirgo*
in an early inscription and *guberno* from the Greek
$\kappa \nu \beta \epsilon \rho \nu \hat{\omega}$. The disuse of K was perhaps aided by the
custom of writing it I⟨, which was liable to be confounded
with I C.

For a time F (F) and V (*v*) were employed pro-
miscuously to express the *w*-sound (con-
F, V.   sonantal *u*) of such words as *uinum*, *uicus*,
a sound which, though the symbol for it remained in their
alphabet, the Greeks of Italy had practically ceased to
pronounce. During this time the *bilabial* (not, as in
English, *labiodental*) *f*-sound, which was unknown to
Greek, was represented in Latin by FH, i.e. F*h* (e.g.
FHEFHAKED = *fefaced* = *fecit*, see p. 105). As time

went on, however, V was confined to *u*, consonantal or otherwise, and thus the H in FH became superfluous and was finally dropped.

Greek Z probably represented in the alphabets of Cumae and Naples the *z*-sound ('soft' *s*) in Eng. *has, maze*. In early times this sound was part of the Latin language, but later changed to *r*, and Z went out of use, while G, a modification of C, took its place in the Alphabet with the value (*g*). These latter reforms were ascribed to Appius Claudius Caecus, the censor of 312 B.C., who did for the Latin Alphabet what Archinus did for the Attic Alphabet in the archonship of Eucleides (403). He established the official Alphabet of 21 letters as follows:

A B C D E F G H I K L M N O P Q R S T V X,

with the values we now give them, save that 'I' did duty for both *i* and *j* (i.e. *i*-vowel and *i*-consonant), and similarly V represented both *u* and *v* (i.e. *u*-vowel and *u*-consonant).

Z, G.

App. Claudius' Official Alphabet.

Traces of the older Alphabet remained in—

the use of K in a few words, e.g. *Kalendae, Kaeso, Karthago*;

the use of C and CN as abbreviations for *Gaius* and *Gnaeus* respectively;

the abbreviation M' for *Manius*, a survival of the early five-stroke M (⋀)[1].

The letters Y and Z, representing *υ* and *ζ*, came into use in the time of Cicero in writing Greek loan-words, e.g. *zona, cymba*, previously written (e.g. by Plautus) *sona, cumba*. The same spelling was extended to a few words such as *lacryma, inclytus,*

Greek letters.

[1] See the Praenestine Fibula, page 105.

wrongly supposed to be derived from Greek. At the same period it became customary to write *Corinthus* for the older *Corintus*, *Achilles* for *Acilles*, *Rhodus* for *Rodus*, etc.

Among other modifications, we may notice the doubling of consonants which were sounded double (introduced by Ennius about 205 B.C.), the doubling of long vowels when their position left their 'natural' length uncertain, e.g. *paastores* (introduced by Accius about 130), and the writing of *ei* for long *i*. Of these the first reform only was permanent. The second was soon dropped, and the third persisted till the beginning of the Empire.

Other
modifications.

Further changes belong rather to the history of the Language than to that of the Alphabet, and are discussed in the following chapter, where examples of early Latin inscriptions will be found.

The most important inscription of the Classical period is the *Monumentum Ancyranum*, or *Res Gestae Diui Augusti*, inscribed upon the wall of a temple at Ancyra in Galatia. This and other inscriptions of the period are now taken as examples of the spelling of Classical Latin, and it is largely by their means that modern editors have purged our Classical texts of the medieval orthography which had crept into them. This may be seen by comparing any modern text with the editions of a century or two centuries ago, or with the Latin of the epitaphs in our old churches, where we find such forms as *charissima, lachrymæ, conjugis*, for *carissima, lacrimae* (or *lacrymae*), *coniugis*. The letters of the Monument are the same as our own capitals, save that I stands for *i* or *i̯* (y), and V for *u* or *u̯* (w).

Mon. Ancyr.

The subsequent history of the Alphabet must not detain us long. In the early Empire the Romans developed out of the capitals a *cursive* hand, in the same way as the Hieratic was developed out of the Hieroglyphic in Egypt. As written books multiplied, this hand was gradually improved. The letters became simplified, and abbreviations were introduced by monkish scribes. About 450 A.D. it was introduced by St Patrick from Gaul into Ireland, whence it was carried by Irish monks into Northumbria. When Alcuin of York founded the school of Tours in the reign of Charlemagne (800) he introduced his native script. This writing of Tours is known, from *Charlemagne*, as 'the Caroline Minuscule,' i.e. small letters. About this time *j* began to be differentiated from *i* and *v* from *u*, while 'double-*u*' (or, as the French call it, 'double-*v*'), vv, was introduced for the *w*-sound. In the 12th century the Caroline Minuscule degenerated into the 'Black Letter,' ·in which the earliest printed books (1460) were produced, and from which modern German print is descended. In the early part of the 16th century, however, the 'Roman' letters founded on the old Caroline Minuscule superseded the Black Letter type in England, while our handwriting, which had hitherto resembled that of modern Germany (cf. old Church Registers), began to be modelled on the new 'Italian' style derived from the same source. With the exception of the abolition (about 1800) of the old *f*-like *s* at the beginning or in the middle of a word, the English Alphabet has practically undergone no further change.

Subsequent history of the Alphabet.

Cursive.

Caroline Minuscule.

j, v, w.

Black Letter.

Roman Type.

CHAPTER V.

THE ARYAN LANGUAGE AND ITS DESCENDANTS.

Earlier Theories—Modern Theory—Linguistic and Racial Descent—
European Races—'Cradle' of Aryan Language—Pre-Aryan
Affinities—Table of Aryan Languages—Table of Affinities of
Aryan Languages — Indo-Iranian — Armenian — Greek —
Albanian— Italic— Celtic—Germanic—Letto-Slavonic—Date of
Undivided Aryan—*History of Greek*—The Dialects—Aeolic—
Doric—Ionic—Attic and its Descendants—Loan-words in Greek
—*History of Latin*—Praenestine Fibula—Sctum de Bac.—
Early Writers—Written and Spoken Latin—Graffiti—Petronius
—Vulgar Latin after 300 A.D.—Oscan and Umbrian—Loan-words
in Latin—Historical Classification of Latin—*History of French*
—Romance—Why do we not speak Romance ?—Differentiation
of Romance—Langue d'oc and Langue d'oïl—Norman French—
French of Paris—Standard French—*History of English*—The
Britons — Latin loan-words — The English Invaders — The
Dialects—Celtic elements—Church-Latin—Scandinavian ele-
ments — French — 'Learned' Latin — Standard English —
Historical Division—Sweet's Three Stages—Spoken and Written
English—Loan-words in English—'True' English and adopted
words.

TILL the end of the 18th century Latin was held to
have been derived from a dialect of Greek,
Earlier
theories.
or Greek and Latin to be cousins, both
derived from Hebrew. When Sanskrit, the

language of the Brahman Scriptures, was made known to
European scholars by Sir William Jones in 1786, it became
obvious that Greek and Latin were closely allied to
Sanskrit. Later, upon the discovery of Zend, the ancient
Persian language of the Holy Book of the Zoroastrians,

The Modern
Theory.

a comparison of the four languages made
certain his conception of a great family of
sister-languages descended from a single
parent. Such a phenomenon is exactly parallel to the
descent of the Romance languages—French, Italian,
Spanish, and others—from Latin, save that in their case
the parent-language has been preserved in literature and
inscriptions, while the common original of Latin, Greek,
Sanskrit, and Zend has to be reconstructed from its
descendants. To take an illustration from another science:
if we wished to reconstruct the original horse from which
it is conceived that all existing horses are descended, we
might compare the following data:

(1)   The different varieties of living horse, e.g. Arab,
        Shetland ;

(2)   Fossil remains of extinct varieties, e.g. the
        American toed horse ;

(3)   Ancient representations in art, e.g. the horses
        of the Parthenon Frieze.

In the same way we may reconstruct this parent-
language of most European and some Asiatic languages
by comparing

(1)   Different varieties of living languages, e.g. spoken
        English and German ;

(2)   Dead languages preserved in their literature, e.g.
        Greek and Latin ;

(3)   Dead languages preserved in inscriptions, e.g. the
        Old Persian of the cuneiform inscriptions.

In the following examples from five languages (and throughout the succeeding Chapters) Greek and Latin should be pronounced as we have indicated in Chapter IV., and Sanskrit and other less familiar languages according to the phonetic notation used throughout this book (see Index of Phonetic Symbols).

Examples of Cognates.

English	German	Latin	Greek (Doric)	Sanskrit
mother (Old Eng. *mōdor*)	*Mutter*	*māter*	μάτηρ	*mātár*
two (once pronounced as spelt)	*zwei*	*duo*	δύο	*dváu*
sta-nd	*ste-hen*	*stā-re*	ἱστᾱμι (for σἱ-στᾱ-μι)	*ti-ṣṭʰā-mi*
bear	*bär-en*	*fer-ō*	φέρ-ω	*bʰár-āmi*

From these *and many others* we may gather that the sounds of the parent-words were those represented by the symbols *mātēr, dwō* (or *dẏō*), *stistāmi, bʰerō*.

The hypothetic language whose reconstruction we have thus exemplified is known variously as Indo-European, Indo-Germanic, Eurasian, and Aryan. The last name is employed in this book.

Names of the Parent-Language.

It must not be supposed that every original Aryan word is found in every language of the Aryan family with the same meaning. The words for 'mother' and 'two' are particularly favourable to preservation of meaning; but, in the majority of cases, cognate or related words—or, as we might say, Aryan words in English, German, Latin, and other, dress—are found to have developed or preserved different meanings just as they have developed or preserved different modes of inflexion (see the following Chapter). Even in the short list given above under *stand*,

Variations of Meaning.

we find that Greek, for instance, developed or preserved
not only a reduplication σι- (modified into ἱ-) and an inflexion -μι, but also a transitive meaning 'set,' thus
differing from English, German, and Latin[1]. It is the
business of Comparative Philology to explain how these
changes arose.

It is necessary here to warn the student against the
common mistake of supposing a linguistic
descent to be identical with a descent by birth.
Linguistic
Descent.
For instance, when the Romans conquered
Gaul, their *language* gradually ousted the original language
of the Gauls (which was something like modern Welsh);
but a Roman *population* did not at the same time replace
a Gallic population. The people of Gaul remained largely
as they were, but gradually came to speak a different
language. Thus when we speak of an Aryan race we
mean the race who spoke the language from which these
languages, English, German, Latin, Greek, Sanskrit, etc.,
are derived; we do not mean a race from whom the
English, Germans, Romans, Greeks, Hindus, etc. might
be descended by blood. It is even possible that the Aryan
race has entirely died out.

By race the ancient inhabitants of Europe may be
arranged into four classes:
Classifica-
tion of
Europeans
by Race.
(1) The Scandinavians, a *tall* Northern
long-headed race, the people who formed the
kitchen-middens or shell-mounds of Den-
mark; now represented by the Swedes, the Frisians, and
the fair North Germans.

(2) The Iberians, the *short*, swarthy, Southern *long*-
headed race, whose remains are found in the *long* barrows

---

[1] In early Latin, however, *stāre* was transitive.

of Britain and the sepulchral caves of France and Spain ;
now represented by some of the Welsh and Irish, the
Corsicans, and the Spanish Basques. Their affinities are
African.

(3) The Celts, a *tall* Northern *short*-headed race,
the people of the lake-dwellings of Switzerland, whose
remains are found in the *round* barrows of Britain,
and in Belgian, French, and Danish graves ; they
were florid, with light eyes and red hair, and are now
represented by the Danes, the Slavs, and some of the
Irish. Their affinities are Ugrian (see below).

(4) The Ligurians, the *short*, Alpine, *short*-headed
race, whose remains are found in Belgian caves and
in central France; they were black-haired, and are now
represented by the people of Auvergne, Savoy, and
Switzerland. Their affinities are Lapp and Finnic.

Of these four races it is probable, from many considerations, that either the Scandinavians (1) or the
Celts (3) were the actual Aryan race. If the former, it
would seem that Scandinavia was the original home of the
Aryan language, if the latter, Lithuania.

It is possible, however, that some day we may go still
further back and prove (1) Aryan, (2) Ugrian,
Pre-Aryan
Affinities.
the parent-language of two other families
represented by Finnish and Hungarian, (3)
Altaic, the original of Turkish, and possibly (4) Japanese,
to be descended from a common ancestor. There is
moreover another claimant to affinity with the Aryan
family, Sumerian or Accadian, the most ancient language
of which any records have been preserved. This language
was spoken in the valley of the Euphrates, and was
beginning to be a dead language in 2000 B.C. Its earliest
inscriptions go back to 8000 B.C. It has been found to

bear striking affinities to the Ugrian family. Thus it may be possible to draw up some such scheme as this:

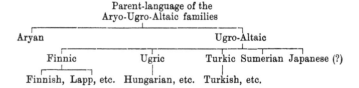

If the affinities here indicated prove on investigation to be correct, it will follow that the Aryans were an off-shoot of an Asiatic race, and that they invaded Scandinavia or Lithuania and imposed their higher civilisation and language on the pre-historic Stone-Age population, the resulting mixed race gradually reverting under climatic influence to the type of the original inhabitants.

We are at present, however, concerned only with Aryan.

At page 92, where it is placed for convenience of reference, will be found a table which includes the principal languages of the family, and may be taken as a *rough indication* of their descent. It must be borne in mind that we have here only those which survive either as living languages in the speech of to-day, or as dead languages in literature, inscriptions, etc., and that many languages (e.g. Thracian and Scythian), which might have considerably modified the grouping, have been wholly or almost wholly lost.

Table of Aryan Languages.

The table shows about 60 languages, 25 of which are dead and 35 living. The latter are shaded. It must not be imagined that all the ovals include actual languages. For instance, Germanic is the name for a group of languages, not a language; it is probable that there was one original offshoot of Aryan from which the Germanic languages are all derived, but, as in the case of parent-Aryan, there are no records of it.

The affinities of the various groups may be better
represented thus, the unshaded portions
Table of   representing languages which have not sur-
Affinities.   vived, but which doubtless formed intermediate links.

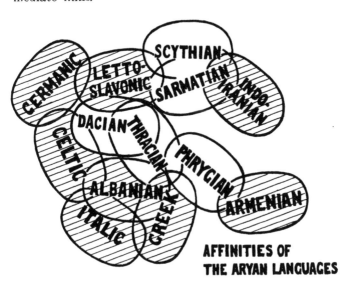

**AFFINITIES OF
THE ARYAN LANGUAGES**

Italic has greater affinity to Celtic on the one hand and Greek on the other than it has to Germanic or Letto-Slavonic. Greek is more closely allied with Italic than with Celtic or Germanic[1].

As will be seen from these tables, there are eight primary groups of Aryan languages—Indo-Iranian, Armenian, Greek, Albanian, Italic, Celtic, Germanic, and

[1] The diagram is practically that of Dr Isaac Taylor, *Origin of the Aryans*, p. 269.

Letto-Slavonic. Philologists who employ other names for the original language apply the name of Aryan to the Indo-Iranian group.

I. INDO-IRANIAN:

   (a) Indian branch:—
     (1) Sanskrit: the ancient language of the Punjab, preserved in the Veda or Holy Scriptures of the Brahmans, which were handed down for centuries by oral tradition before being committed to writing, and date probably from about 1500 B.C.
     (2) Prakrit: ⎫
     (3) Pali: ⎬ dialects of Sanskrit, now dead.
     (4) Hindi: ⎫
     (5) Gujarati: ⎪ the modern representatives of
     (6) Bengali ⎨   Prakrit and Pali.
       and others: ⎭

The Gipsy language belongs to this group.

   (b) Iranian branch:—
     (1) Zend (or Old Bactrian): the language of the Avesta or Bible of the Zoroastrians, dating probably from 1100 to 600 B.C.
     (2) Old Persian: the language of the cuneiform inscriptions of the Euphrates valley; the oldest belong to the reign of Darius, 520 B.C.
     (3) Modern Persian: derived from Old Persian. Its literature begins about 950 A.D., and includes the poems of Omar Khayyám, who wrote about 1100.

II. ARMENIAN: known from 400 A.D. It has no immediate living cognates, but is probably to be connected with ancient Phrygian, of which some inscriptions survive.

III. GREEK: known since the time of the Homeric poems (9th century B.C.?). Strictly speaking it is a group of languages classed as Ionic, Attic, Doric, and Aeolic[1]. From Attic, Modern Greek or Romaic has been developed.

IV. ALBANIAN: the language of ancient Illyricum. It is now spoken in Albania, the westernmost province of Turkey. It has no early literature, and, like Armenian, it stands by itself.

V. ITALIC: a group comprising the chief languages of Italy.

    (1)   Oscan: ⎫ known only from inscriptions,
    (2)   Umbrian[2]: ⎬ place-names, e.g. *Pompeii*, and
                 ⎭ names of Romans, e.g. *Pontius*.

    (3) Latin: known by inscriptions from about 400 B.C. Vulgar Latin, which even in the time of Augustus differed considerably from Literary Latin, is known later as Popular Latin, and is now represented by the Romance languages—French, Provençal, Italian, Portuguese, Spanish, Roumansch, and Roumanian (see p. 113).

    In many respects the Italic group bears a great affinity to the Celtic.

VI. CELTIC: a group comprising the languages of the extreme west of Europe.

    (*a*) Gaulish: known only from inscriptions, names, etc.; the language of the Gauls conquered by Caesar.

    (*b*) Goidelic: these three languages were probably identical as late as 900 A.D.; when the Scots from Ireland conquered the Picts, who were the inhabitants of Scotland

---

[1] And others. See p. 94.

[2] These are the most important Italic languages other than Latin. There are others (see p. 104).

in Roman times, the language of the Picts became extinct;
it may have been a dialect of Gaulish:—

(1)   Irish : known from inscriptions of the 6th
and 7th centuries, glosses upon Latin MSS. of the 8th
century, and a literature extending to modern times.
Still spoken in parts of Ireland.

(2)   Manx : still spoken in the Isle of Man.

(3)   Gaelic (or Scotch Gaelic) : known from the
11th century ; the language of the Highlands of Scotland
(not to be confused with the Lowland Scotch, e.g. of
Burns, which is a dialect of Old English).

(c)   Cymric :—

(1)   Welsh : the literature of this language ex-
tends from the 11th century.

(2)   Cornish : became extinct about 1800, but
survives in a literature dating from about 1500.

(3)   Breton (or Armorican) : the language of
Brittany ; an offshoot of Cornish about 500 A.D.

VII.   GERMANIC (or Teutonic) : comprising Gothic
and two sub-groups.

(a)   Gothic : preserved in a West Gothic (Visigothic)
version of the New Testament made by bishop Ulfilas
about 350 A.D., which is the earliest record of the
Germanic group.

(b)   The West Germanic branch, comprising :—

(1)   Old High[1] German (first in epic fragments
dating from before 800 A.D.), with its descendant Modern
German,

(2)   Old Low[1] German, subdivided into

(i)   Old Saxon : dating from the 9th century,
with its modern non-literary representative Low Saxon,
which is spoken over a large part of Northern Germany,

---

[1] See footnote, p. 117.

(ii) Anglo-Frisian: the common original of Modern Frisian and English (see p. 116), of which the earliest monument is the poem *Beowulf*, which may have been composed before the English invasion of Britain; Frisian is spoken in the north of Holland and on the N.W. coast of Germany, and is known collectively with Low Saxon as Plattdeutsch,

(iii) Old Low Franconian: the language of the Franks, whence come Dutch and Flemish.

(c) The Scandinavian (or East Germanic) branch: these four languages were probably identical till 800 A.D., the old language being preserved in Runic inscriptions from about 400; in the 9th century the language began to diverge into two dialects, East and West, which became further differentiated before 1100:—

(1) East Scandinavian, comprising

(i) Danish: the language of modern Denmark and Norway,

(ii) Swedish: the language of all Sweden except the extreme north, where Lappish and Finnish (non-Aryan, see p. 86) are spoken.

The earliest monuments of East Scandinavian are Runic inscriptions dating from about 950. Swedish literature begins about 1250.

(2) West Scandinavian, comprising

(i) Icelandic: the language of the Eddas and the Sagas (800—1150), known as Modern Icelandic since 1540,

(ii) Norse or Old Norwegian: now represented only by peasants' dialects[1].

---

[1] Modern Norwegian, the language of educated Norway, is really Danish, but has adopted many Old Norwegian words since the political separation from Denmark in 1814. There are also some marked differences of pronunciation.

VIII. LETTO-SLAVONIC:

(*a*) Lettic or Baltic branch: a group comprising the languages spoken on the southern and south-eastern shores of the Baltic:—

(1) Old Prussian: became extinct about 1700, leaving a catechism and a glossary as the only literature of this group.

(2) Lithuanian : ⎫ spoken in the frontier district
(3) Lettish :   ⎭ of Russia and Prussia.

(*b*) Slavonic branch: comprising the languages (except Turkish and Hungarian, which are non-Aryan, see p. 85) of Central and Eastern Europe:—

(1) West Slavonic, subdivided into

(i) Wendish: spoken in a district of Central Germany,

(ii) Czechish or Bohemian: the language of Bohemia; its earliest records are ecclesiastical writings dating from about 950 A.D.,

(iii) Polish: the language of Poland; its earliest literature is prior to 1200.

(2) Old Bulgarian (or East Slavonic): preserved in the earliest Christian writings of the Slavs dating from about 900 A.D., with its offshoots

(i) Slovenian: spoken in parts of Austria and Hungary,

(ii) Russian: of which the literature begins about 1050,

(iii) Servo-Croatian: spoken in Servia and on the north-eastern coast of the Adriatic, dating from about 1150,

(iv) Modern Bulgarian: of which there is a considerable literature, consisting largely of collections of popular songs.

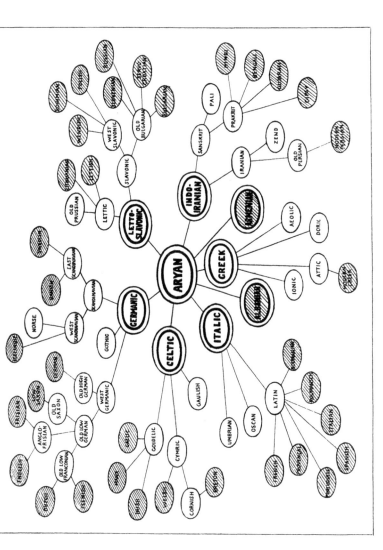

TABLE ILLUSTRATING THE DESCENT OF THE PRINCIPAL ARYAN LANGUAGES. (See p. 86.)

To face p. 92]

As to the age of these languages, the oldest contemporary records, apart from the still un-
*Date of undi-
vided Aryan.* deciphered Cretan writings, are the Greek
and Italic inscriptions. These do not go
much further back than 600 or 700 B.C. The oldest
literary document, the Rig-Veda, may be as old as
1500 B.C. A rough estimate based on the comparison
of the oldest forms of each language gives us about
10,000 B.C. as the latest date for an undivided Aryan
language, i.e. the latest date at which all Aryan speakers
could understand each other[1].

The questions, Why are these languages different, and
how did they become so? will be discussed in the following
Chapter. We may, however, discuss briefly the history of
the languages with which we are chiefly concerned.

According to a recent ethnological work the Greeks of
the Homeric Age were a composite race,
*History of
Greek.* a mixture of the old Pelasgian stock with
the Achaean invaders from the north. Both
Pelasgians and Achaeans spoke an Aryan language, but
the language which prevailed and which we know as
Greek was the language of the Pelasgians.

In the historic period we find this language represented by a group of dialects spoken in Southern Italy,
Sicily, Greece, the Aegean, the Western coast of Asia
Dialects. Minor, Cyrene, and Cyprus. The affinities
of these dialects are Latin on the one hand
and Indo-Iranian on the other. They differ in their
sounds, inflexion, syntax, and vocabulary. They may be
broadly divided into two groups,

[1] Sweet, *Hist. of Language Primer.*

(1) those which preserve the original Aryan $\bar{a}$ (as in μάτηρ), and

(2) those which change it to $\bar{e}$ (as in μήτηρ), and are generally classed as follows:—

$\bar{a}$ {

(i) Aeolic: corresponding to the Achaean race-group, spoken chiefly in Thessaly (except Phthiotis), Boeotia, Lesbos, and N.W. Asia Minor.

(ii) Doric: corresponding to the Dorian race-group originally living north of the Gulf of Corinth but migrating later into the Peloponnese; spoken chiefly in Laconia and Tarentum, Messenia, Argolis and Aegina, Megara with Selinus and Byzantium, Corinth with Corcyra and Syracuse, Crete, Melos and Thera with Cyrene, and Rhodes with Gela and Agrigentum.

η {

(iii) Ionic: corresponding to the Ionian race-group, spoken in Euboea with Cumae and Chalcidice, the Cyclades, Chios and Samos, and S.W. Asia Minor including Ephesus and Miletus.

(iv) Attic: the dialect of Attica, classed by some writers as Ionic, but showing important differences.

To these four classes should be added several smaller groups and single dialects, which, though they all preserve the original $\bar{a}$, cannot be assigned with certainty to any one of them:—

Arcadian and Cyprian,
Pamphylian,

Elean,

the dialects of N.W. Greece—Achaea, Locris, Phocis (with Delphi), Aetolia, Acarnania, Phthiotis, and Epirus.

(i) Apart from inscriptions Aeolic is represented by the Lyric Fragments of Alcaeus and Sappho, where its chief peculiarities are seen in—

Aeolic.

the absence of the rough breathing,

a more general use of -μι-verbs (e.g. κάλη101μι = καλέω),

the retention of ϝ (w),

certain vowels (e.g. -ως = -ους in the Acc. Plural),

the labialisation of dentals under certain circumstances (e.g. φήρ for θήρ, πέτταρες or πέσυρες for τέτταρες). Aeolic also threw back the accent as far as possible, e.g. σόφος, αὗτος, πόταμος.

For an example of Aeolic see the quotation below (p. 97) from the 'original' Iliad.

(ii) Doric is represented in literature by the Lyric Fragments of Alcman, the treaty in Thucydides v. 77, the Laconian in the *Lysistrata*, 1076 ff., and the Megarian in the *Acharnians*, 729 ff. Aristophanes, however, is considered untrustworthy. The Doric of Theocritus is a more or less artificial literary dialect, and does not truly represent the dialect of any one district. In the choruses of Attic tragedy the Doric forms (e.g. μάτηρ for μήτηρ) are a literary convention. Among the universal characteristics of Doric we may notice—

Doric.

-μες for -μεν in the 1st Person Plural, e.g. λύομες for λύομεν (cf. Latin *regimus*),

the Future Passive has the Active Suffix, e.g. λυθήσω for λυθήσομαι,

the Aorist and Future of verbs in -ζω are formed
with -ξ- (e.g. καθίζω, καθίξω),

λάω is used for ' wish.'

In Laconian Doric notable points are—

τιρ for τις,

μῶά for μοῦσα,

σ for θ, e.g. ναὶ τὼ σίω = νὴ τὼ θεώ (though this is
probably later than Alcman, Thucydides, and Aristophanes,
where the change is thought to be due to copyists).

In Sicilian Doric we find—

ν for λ before dentals, e.g. ἦνθον for ἦλθον,

Perfects declined as Presents, e.g. πεπόνθεις = πέ-
πονθας.

Theocritus in his Bucolic idylls, as we have them now,
shows these forms; some of his forms, however, are Aeolic,
e.g. μοῖσαι, νίκημι.

In Cretan Doric we find the original -ns preserved,
e.g. τόνς = τούς, θένς = θείς.

(iii) Ionic is represented by an extensive literature,
which must be dealt with more at length.
Ionic.
It may be divided historically thus :—

(1) Old Ionic of the Iliad and the Odyssey (see
below),

(2) Middle Ionic of the Elegiac Poets, e.g.
Mimnermus,

(3) New Ionic of Herodotus and Hippocrates.

The dialect of the Homeric poems (the so-called Epic)
is usually classed as Old Ionic. The ques-
Homer.
tion of its origin is practically the question
of the origin of the poems themselves. This question
has never been conclusively answered. As we have
them now, the Iliad and the Odyssey are mainly Ionic;

but there is a strong admixture of Aeolic forms. The composite nature of their dialect, combined with other considerations, makes it probable that they were either (1) originally composed in Aeolic, or (2) based upon the lays of Aeolic bards. The former view is that of Fick. According to him the Iliad and the Odyssey were composed in Aeolic and have been gradually Ionicised by being handed down by generations of speakers of the Ionic dialect, if they are not actually the result of an early Ionic recension.

The Aeolic Homer.

The Iliad, according to Fick, probably began thus:

μᾶνιν ἄειδε, θέα, Πηληϊάδα' 'Αχίλησς
ὀλλομέναν, ἃ μύρι' 'Αχαίοισ' ἄλγε' ἔθηκε,
πόλλαις δ' ἰφθίμοις ψύχαις Ἄϝιδι προΐαψε...

Our Ionicised version reads as follows:

μῆνιν ἄειδε, θεά, Πηληϊάδεω 'Αχιλῆος
οὐλομένην, ἣ μυρί' 'Αχαιοῖς ἄλγε' ἔθηκε,
πολλὰς δ' ἰφθίμους ψυχὰς Ἄϊδι προΐαψεν...

Notice the hiatus, Πηληϊάδεω 'Αχιλῆος, which has been produced by the change of dialect.

The other view is as follows:—The Iliad is the result of the work of a great Ionian poet and his school upon Aeolian material. This material consisted of Aeolic lays embodying the legends of Achilles, Agamemnon, and other heroes. If we take the date of the first great poet as about 900— 850 B.C., the Iliad had probably grown into something like its present shape before about 750. With regard to the Odyssey, its kernel, the 'Return of Odysseus,' arose in a similar way and was afterwards enlarged by the addition first (before about 800) of most of the later books, and later (before about 650) of the first four.

The Ionic Homer.

With regard to Hesiod, Fick's view is that he wrote
Hesiod. in the dialect of Delphi and that his poems
were assimilated later to the 'Epic' style,
i.e. Ionicised Aeolic. It is more probable that Hesiod
himself wrote in 'Epic,' as the only literary style he
knew. He is generally considered to be responsible for
the nucleus of the *Works and Days*, which is probably
to be dated between 750 and 700 B.C. The *Theogony* is
of different authorship and somewhat later date. The
Shield of Heracles may be as old as 600, but
The Homeric is probably not older. Some of the Homeric
Hymns. Hymns belong to this period.

Between Homer and Hesiod on the one hand and
Middle Ionic. Herodotus and Hippocrates on the other
comes the Ionic of the poets Archilochus,
Mimnermus, Hippōnax, and others. In their fragments
we find a certain admixture of Epic forms, which to them
were literary archaisms, e.g. we find θανάτοιο as well as
θανάτου, γαῖα as well as γῆ.

It is characteristic of Ionic (as also of Attic) to change
original ā into ē, to drop ϝ (w), and to use ἄν not κεν or
κα. A characteristic which it does not share with Attic,
κο- and κη- for πο- and πη- (representing Aryan q^wo-
and $q^wā$-), e.g. κοῦ = ποῦ, though frequent in Herodotus
and the Iambic Poets, is found neither in the writings of
Hippocrates nor in inscriptions. Ionic also has no dual.

New Ionic. The chief peculiarities of Herodotus, as we
have him now, are—

η for ā, even where the ā is original, e.g.
πρῆγμα,

κ for π as above,

ξεῖνος, μοῦνος, etc. for ξένος, μόνος, etc.,

vowels remain uncontracted, e.g. ἐποίεε.

(iv) Attic. The *literature* of Athens was originally

Attic.
Old.

a branch of Ionic literature. The dialect of Solon's fragments is largely Ionic. In the Old Attic of Thucydides and the Tragedians we find relics of this literary tradition in forms borrowed from the Ionic dialect, e.g. ξύν for σύν, αἰεί for ἀεί, θάρσος for θάρρος, and, where required by metre, -οισι, -αισι, in the Dative Plural for -οις, -αις. The other point of difference between Old and New Attic, -σσ- for -ττ-, was probably merely a different spelling of the same sound (Eng. *th* in *thin* doubled, see p. 47). It should be borne in mind that all the above forms were

New.

foreign to *spoken* Attic. The New Attic is seen in Aristophanes, Plato, and Demosthenes. Of this examples are unnecessary.

The Attic dialect and its descendants may be classified

Classification of its descendants.

historically thus (Classical and Post-Classical representing Pagan Greek, then a Transition period, and finally Neo-Hellenic representing Christian Greek[1]):

CLASSICAL:—

(1) B.C. 500–400, Old Attic of Thucydides and the Tragedians.

(2) 400–300, New Attic of Plato and Demosthenes.

POST-CLASSICAL :—

(3) 300–150, Hellenistic.
(a) Alexandrian Prose.
(b) Colloquial.

[1] The Table is practically that of Jannaris's *Historical Greek Grammar*.

(4) 150 B.C.–300 A.D., Graeco-Roman.
    (a) *Atticising*[1]: Lucian and Pau-
        sanias.
    (b) Common or Conventional (ἡ κοινὴ
        διάλεκτος): Polybius and the
        Septuagint.
    (c) Levantine: New Testament.
                         (d) Colloquial[2].

TRANSITIONAL:—

(5) 300–600, Transitional.
    (a) Ecclesiastical (founded on LXX.
        and N.T.).
    (b) Secular (*Atticising*[1]).
                         (c) Colloquial.

NEO-HELLENIC:—

(6) 600–1000, Byzantine.
    (a) Ecclesiastical (combining (a) and
        (b) of previous period).
                         (b) Colloquial.

(7) 1000–1450, Medieval.
    (a) Literary (founded on Colloquial
        of previous period).
                         (b) Colloquial.

(8) 1450–1800, Modern.
    (a) Literary.
                         (b) Colloquial.

(9) 1800–1900, Present.
    (a) Literary (includingJournalistic);
        Atticising[1].
                         (b) Colloquial.

---

[1] i.e. reverting to the Classical Attic models.

[2] Preserved to some extent in Papyri.

The intellectual ascendancy of Athens, coupled with the new need of a common tongue, brought about in the Macedonian period the supremacy of her dialect in the eastern Mediterranean. This Hellenistic dialect, as it is called, must have differed considerably according as it was written or spoken.

Hellenistic.

In the Graeco-Roman period we may distinguish, besides the colloquial or spoken dialect (preserved to some extent in 'unlearned' inscriptions and papyri), three dialects,

Graeco-Roman.

(1) that of the Atticising purists such as Lucian, who reverted to Classical Attic models,

(2) a sort of Colonial Greek employed by Hellenised foreigners and Asiatic Greeks, known as the Levantine dialect and seen in the New Testament,

and (3) midway between these two, the Common or Conventional dialect, ἡ κοινὴ διάλεκτος, preserved in the Septuagint, Polybius, and Plutarch.

ἡ κοινή.

In the Period of Transition between Pagan and Christian Greek (300–600 A.D.), ecclesiastical writers founded their style on the Septuagint and the New Testament, while the Secular books revert once more to Classical models.

Later History.

At the beginning of the Neo-Hellenic Period (600–1900) we find the Byzantine Greek which sprang up in the Eastern Empire combining the Ecclesiastical and Secular elements.

In the subdivision of this known as the Medieval Period (1000–1450) there was a great change. Hitherto the language of the people, which though doubtless affected to some extent by the Church language had by this time diverged widely from the ancient dialect, had been rigorously excluded from literature. In this period the literary dialect is for the first time founded on *Colloquial* Greek.

The period of Turkish supremacy (1450–1800) was one of darkness and ignorance, and the Greek language lost all the words belonging to science and culture. The structure remained the same, but the vocabulary was much reduced and changed.

Within the last 80 years the regeneration of Greece and the revival of national spirit has caused much of this loss to be made good. Scholars and journalists, indeed, have imitated the Classical models with such zeal that the dialect of literature and the newspapers is but a modernised form of ancient Attic, unintelligible to the great bulk of the people. The spoken language, however, despite the purists, remains a direct and natural development of the language of Periclean Athens.

Present Greek.

The foreign element in Classical Greek is very small. Among the 5000 words of which (neglecting derivatives and compounds) the language is composed, there are about 70 foreign or presumably foreign words of ordinary occurrence in literature. Of these about 20 occur first in Homer, about 40 in the writers of the 7th, 6th, and 5th centuries especially Herodotus, and the rest in the writers of the 4th century and later.

Loan-words in Greek.

(1) Homer:—

Metals: κασσίτερος[8], χρυσός[8], σίδηρος, and μό-λυβδος[1].

---

[1] Only in the word μολύβδαινα.

Other merchandise: ἐλέφας (ivory), ὀθόνη[S], φοῖνιξ[S], and κρόκος[S].

Miscellaneous: πέλεκυς[S], χιτών[S], φῦκος[S], κίων[S], κάνεον[S], κυπάρισσος[S], ἀσάμινθος, ἄφλαστον, ἔθειρα, πεσσός, λέων.

(2) The 7th, 6th, and 5th centuries:—

Spices: κασία[S], κίνναμον[S], κύμινον[S], λιβανωτός[S], μύρρα[S], νᾶπυ.

Other merchandise: ἑλλέβορος, σήσαμον, κάνναβις[A], φάσηλος, κόμμι, νίτρον[S], γύψος[A], ἄσφαλτος, σινδών[A], βίβλος, χάρτης, ἔβενος[S], σμάραγδος[S].

Money: μνᾶ[S], δαρεικός[A].

Miscellaneous: σάνδαλον[A], σάκκος[S], σισύρα, ἀρραβών[S], κάδος[S], κόφινος, βάρβιτος, λύρα, διθύραμβος, ἔλεγος, ἄκατος, ἀσκάντης, κόλυμβος, τέρμινθος, μάγος[A], βάσανος, ἀτταγᾶς, κάμηλος[S], πάνθηρ[A], σέρφος, ταῶς[A], τίγρις[A].

(3) The 4th century and later:—

Precious stones: ἴασπις[S], σάπφειρος[S], μαργαρίτης[A].

Spices: βάλσαμον[S], νάρδος[S], πέπερι[A], σίναπι, χαλβάνη[S].

Miscellaneous: γάζα[A], πάπυρος.

Of the above words those marked [S] are from Semitic sources, generally having their counterpart in Hebrew; those marked [A] are from Aryan languages other than Greek, e.g. Old Persian (σάνδαλον) and Sanskrit (σινδών). Of the rest βίβλος, χάρτης, πάπυρος, κόμμι, and λέων are Egyptian, and μόλυβδος probably Iberian[1]. The sources of the remaining words are doubtful or unknown.

Their Sources.

---

[1] The pre-Roman language of Spain, now represented by Basque, spoken in the Pyrenees.

After 150 B.C. words had to be found for Roman officers and institutions. For this purpose Greek words were mostly employed with a new signification, e.g. ὕπατος for *consul*, but in some cases Latin words such as σπεκουλάτωρ, πραιτώριον, δηνάριον, came into use. Two interesting importations of this period are σήρ, 'silk,' from the Old Chinese *sir*, and βίσων, 'aurochs,' from an old Germanic language (cf. German *Wisent*).

The language of the Romans was originally, as the name implies, the language of Latium, and *History of Latin.* its early history is parallel to that of Oscan and Umbrian and the other languages of the Italic group. The affinities of these languages are Celtic on the one hand and Greek on the other. Thus Welsh and Latin both make the Passive in -*r*, and *Affinities of Italic.* in Gaulish there was a Dative Plural of the third declension in -*bo*, e.g. *matrebo*=*matribus* (in early poetry *matribu'*).

The earliest records of Latin date from the 5th century B.C. The oldest inscription[1] is that *Praenestine Fibula.* of the Praenestine Fibula (i.e. brooch found at Praeneste), which is generally ascribed to the 5th century. A drawing of it is given opposite. It reads from right to left:

Manios med fhefhaked Numasioi,

i.e. *Manius me fecit Numerio*, 'Manius made me for Numerius.'

---

[1] The inscription found in 1899 in the Comitium at the N.W. corner of the Roman Forum is of extreme interest as by far the oldest *official* Latin document. It is considered to date from before 390, but is probably not so old as the Praenestine Fibula.

Here we should notice—

that the strong stress accent on the first syllable has not yet changed the nominative *-os* (identical with the Greek) into *-us*;

mēd the accusative has the *-d* of the ablative (so too, *ted*, *sed*, are both accusative and ablative, see below); this form is common in Old Latin and was due either to a confusion of the two forms *me*, accusative, and *med*, ablative (so in Eng., *him*, originally the dative as in *give it him*, has ousted the old accusative *hine*) or else to a suffix *-id* found in Sanskrit;

THE PRAENESTINE FIBULA [see p. 104].

in *fhefhaked*, *fh* (i.e. ᚠ*h*) was the early symbol for the bilabial *f*-sound (see p. 78);

-ak- is not yet changed by the stress to *-ek-*, or *-ēd* (representing *-eid*) to *-ĕt* and finally *-it*;

k has not yet given way to *c*;

we have the reduplicated form *fĕfăkei* for *fēcī* (cf. the uncertainty in Classical Latin between *pepigi* and *pegi*);

in *Numasioi*, the accentuation of the first syllable has not weakened the succeeding vowels, i.e. it is not yet *Numesioi*;

we still have *s* representing the 'soft' *s* (z) between vowels, which afterwards became *r* ;

the dative singular -*ōi* has not yet become -*ō*.

A copy of the *Senatus consultum de Bacchanalibus,*
Sctum de Bac.
a decree of 186 B.C., two years before the death of Plautus, has been found on a bronze tablet in Southern Italy, and is invaluable as showing a middle stage in the changes that were going on in the language between the 4th century and the Classical period. It should be borne in mind, however, that legal documents and the like are apt to preserve archaisms (e.g. in this case the -*d* of the ablative, which is proved by contemporary inscriptions not to have been generally pronounced at this time). A short extract must suffice :

Bacas uir nequis adiese uelet ceiuis Romanus neue nominus Latini neue socium quisquam nisei pr urbanum adiesent isque de senatuos sententiad dum ne minus senatoribus c adesent quom ea res cosoleretur iousiset,

which we may rewrite in Classical Latin thus :

Bacchas uir nequis adiisse uellet ciuis Romanus, neue nominis Latini, neue sociorum quisquam, nisi pr(aetorem) urbanum adiissent, isque de senatus sententia, dum ne minus senatoribus c(entum) adessent cum ea res consuleretur, iussisset.

Notice here—

as in earlier inscriptions, there are no double letters, e.g. *adesent, uelet, iousiset* (see p. 79);

Bacas, in Greek words *ch, ph, th* only came in at the close of the Republic (see p. 79);

in *adiese,* -*es*- for -*is*-, probably a relic of the use of *e* for *ei,* cf. *fhefhaked* above ;

in *ceiuis*, *ei* represents long *i*; this custom was just coming in; notice *Latini* not *Lateini* below;

Romanus, contrast this with *Manios* above; the stress-accent has done its work;

nominus is a relic of the -*os*-form of the Aryan genitive; the usual form -*is* comes from -*es*;

in *Latini* (genitive) we have -*i* not -*ei*, which strictly belongs to the nominative plural;

in *socium* we have the correct form of the 2nd declension genitive plural in -*ōm* (cf. Greek -ων) afterwards -*ŏm* (weakened by the stress on the first syllable), preserved in poetry in Classical times, e.g. *deum, diuom*, and in *sestertium, nummum*; the ending -*orum* originated in the pronouns, where it was formed on the analogy of the -*arum* of the *a*-stems;

in *senatuos* we have a bye-form of the 4th declension genitive singular; there seems to have been some doubt how this genitive should be formed, as we find *senati* as well as the Classical *senatūs* and in Terence *Heaut.* 287 we have *anuis* for *anūs*;

sententiad, so in the same inscription *magistratud, preiuatod*; this is the regular form of the ablative singular in -*a*, -*i*, -*o*, and -*u* in Old Latin, and is found in Oscan;

cosoleretur, cos- for *cons-* (cf. abbreviation *cos* for *consul*); this points to the nasalising of the *o* as in French *bon*; the *n* was restored in Classical spelling; -*sol-* has not yet been weakened to -*sul-*; notice the -*r*- where the earlier inscriptions would give -*s*- (cf. *Numasioi* above);

iousiset; there was a bye-form *ioubeo* for *iŭbeo*, of which this is probably the pluperfect subjunctive; the *u* in the Classical *iussi* is short by nature; notice that *ou* has not yet become *ū*.

It will be seen that a large proportion of the above changes are due to stress-accent. This is more fully discussed in Chapter III.

Before the above inscription was written Plautus had produced most of his plays, but these, like the fragments of contemporary writers such as Naevius and Ennius, are less trustworthy than contemporary inscriptions as examples of the Latin of the period. They have come down to us through later Latin, and their text has been to a certain extent modernised. By the help of inscriptions, however, the old forms can be restored where the metre requires it, though Plautus' rules of metre are by no means the same as those which obtained in Classical times.

Evidence of early writers.

Greek is already a collective name for a group of dialects when it emerges from the pre-historic period; Latin, on the other hand, did not develop dialects till it became the language of the various provinces of the Roman Empire. The difference between a dialect and a language is only one of degree. We may therefore consider that Latin bears the same relation to Italic, the hypothetic ancestor of Latin, Oscan, and Umbrian, as Attic Greek to the hypothetic ancestor of Attic, Ionic, Doric, and Aeolic. The ascendancy of Attic over the other Greek dialects was literary, that of Latin over its sister languages mainly political. Though Latin developed no dialects in the ordinary local sense, by the time of Cicero the literary dialect differed considerably from the vernacular. On a leaden bullet dating from 40 B.C. we have the old genitive singular *Caesarus*; cf. *nominus* in the *Sctum de Bac.* Scratched on walls at Pompeii we find (1) *Venere*

Latin and the Greek dialects.

Vulgar Latin Records.

for *Venerem*, pointing to the pronunciation of *-em* as a
Graffiti. nasalised *e* (French *-en*); (2) *libes* for *libens*,
which points to a similar nasalisation (cf.
uicies, uiciens; *uicesimus, uicensimus*; and *cosoleretur* in
the *Sctum de Bac.*); and (3) *cum collegas* for *cum collegis*;
this is the beginning of the loss of the cases (cf. French)
occasioned by the extension of the use of prepositions,
which are less variable and more explicit. There are
indications of the preservation of older forms and older
pronunciation in the speech of the people, just as *thou*
and *thee* are preserved in some English dialects. A striking
uoster. instance is the form *uoster* for the literary
uester; *uoster* was the older form, but as
it belonged to the language of the people it persisted
into Late and Popular Latin and produced the French
votre. We get a glimpse of the vernacular Latin or
Petronius. 'plebeius sermo' of the early Empire in
Petronius, where it is used by certain
characters. Its chief peculiarities are the frequent use
of slang and Greek words and the occurrence of grammatical 'mistakes.' Thus we find—

> *diibus* for *dis*,
> *caelus* for *caelum* (cf. *caeli* plural in Church
> Latin),
> *pudeatur* for *pudeat*,
> *exhortauit* for *exhortatus est*,
> *munus excellente* for *munus excellens*,
> *apoculamus nos* for *abimus ab oculis*,
> *ipsimus* for *dominus*,
> *faciamus* for *bibamus*,
> *saplutus* (ζάπλουτος),
> *tengomenas* (τεγγομένας)

By the time of Ausonius (350 A.D.) the vernacular
and the literary dialect had become almost
Vulgar Latin after 300 A.D. different languages. It is from the vernacular that the Romance languages have
sprung. In the instances given below there is a distinct
approximation, in structure as well as in pronunciation,
to French and Italian. The inscriptions of the time
present the literary language (Low Latin) more or less
correctly according to the education of the
Evidence of Inscriptions. writer, and thus give us glimpses of the
vulgar dialect (Popular Latin) of the period.
But we have no actual record of it.

Here are some of the 'faults':—

instead of the cases we find prepositions used, e.g.
de uino genitive (French *de vin*), *ad uino* dative (French
à vin);

as the result of this extension of the use of prepositions, final consonants are dropped, e.g. *uino* for *uinum*
(Italian *vino*);

auxiliaries such as *habeo, uado,* take the place of tense-
suffixes, e.g. *habeo factum* for *feci* (French *j'ai fait*).

The metre of the hexameter and elegiac epitaphs
of the period is largely a matter of stress
Metre. as in modern English poetry. Two lines
from the epitaph of a Spanish bishop will illustrate this.
It belongs to the early part of the 6th century:

> *te Ioan|nem Tarra|co colu|it mi|rificum | uatem|*
> *tuosque in | hoc lo|co in | pace | condidit | artus|.*

The other Italic languages, of which Oscan and
Umbrian are the most important, are known
Oscan and Umbrian. only from inscriptions, names, and quotations.
Instances of Oscan are—

> pud   = *quod*; cf. ποδ-απός;
> *kumbened* = *conuenit*; cf. *fhefhaked* above;
> *pomtis*   = *quinquies*; cf. πέμπτος;

of Umbrian—

> *pufe*   = *ubi*; cf. *si-cubi*;
> *antakres* = *integris*;
> *futu*   = *esto*; cf. *fui*, φύω.

Latin borrowed a number of words from these languages, e.g. *rufus* beside true Latin *ruber* (both from the Aryan word represented in Greek by ἐρυθρός and in English by *ruddy*) and *popina* beside *coquus*. *Famulus*, too, probably came from this source. We may also compare *Pompeius, Pontius,* with *Quintus, Quinctius* (cf. *pomtis* above). *Nero* is the Sabine cognate of ἀνήρ. The fact that we find *bos* in Latin instead of *uos* for 'ox' (cf. βοῦς, *cow*; *uenio*, βαίνω, *come*) is probably due to its being a loan-word from Oscan.

Loan-words in Latin.

The great majority of loan-words in Latin come from Greek or through Greek. In the writings of Plautus and the contemporary fragments there are about 120 foreign words of ordinary occurrence, nearly all of which are Greek. Greek influence was doubtless felt from very early times. Intercourse with the Greek cities of Southern Italy not only gave the Romans their alphabet, but gradually brought in many words, especially—

(1) those belonging generally to a higher civilisation, e.g. *ballista, balneae, cista, comissor* (κωμίζω = κωμάζω), *cratera, epistola, lampas, lanterna, machina* (μᾱχανᾱ́), *parasitus, poeta* (ποιητής), *purpura, theatrum,* and names of Gods as *Apollo, Hercules, Aesculapius*;

(2) words connected with trade and travel, e.g. *ancora, aplustre* (ἄφλαστον), *carbasus, exanclo* (ἐξαντλέω), *guberno* (κυβερνάω), *mina* (μνᾶ), *talentum, tarpessita* (τραπεζίτης), *thesaurus, trutina* (τρυτάνη).

To these we may add:—

(3) *aer, aether, bracchium, cadus, laena* (χλαῖνα), *pelagus, placenta* (πλακοῦς), *oliuum* (ἔλαιϝον), *rosa* (Aeol. ῥοζά¹), *triumphus* (θρίαμβος).

At the time of the conquest of Greece, the effect of Greek civilisation became still more marked, and the more general study of Greek writers added to Latin literature a large number of words, many of which in course of time became part of the spoken language, e.g.:— *astrum, aula, aura, chorus, coma, glaucus, Musa, philosophus, thalamus²*. By the end of the Augustan period the spoken language, especially in the coast-towns, contained a large proportion of Greek words (see instances above from Petronius).

Foreign names for foreign things naturally came in, as the Roman empire extended, not only from Greece, but from Gaul and Germany and the further East. Such words are:—

balteus, caballus, esseda, petorritum, raeda, sagum, from Celtic, probably Gaulish,

sapo, urus, from Germanic,

piper, sulfur, from Sanskrit.

Plumbum is probably a very early loan-word from Iberian (identical with μόλυβδος, see p. 103), and *tunica* from Semitic (identical with χιτών). *Satelles* is said to be Etruscan.

Latin may be classified historically as follows:—

Historical Classification.

(1) To 250 B.C.: The Preliterary Latin of the early inscriptions,

(2) 250–150: The Early Latin of Plautus and Ennius,

¹ For ῥοδία, i.e. ῥοδέα, a rose-bush.
² Some of these words occur as early as Ennius and Naevius, but it is doubtful how far they were part of the language at that time.

(3) 150–Cicero: Republican Latin,
(4) Cicero–Augustus: Golden Age Latin,
(5) First two centuries of the Empire: Silver Age
      Latin,
(6) 180 A.D.–500: Late Latin.

It should be noted that between periods (3) and (4)
Spoken Latin began to diverge from Literary Latin;
our only glimpses of its earlier history are in Petronius
(60 A.D.) and the 'graffiti' or wall-scribblings of Pompeii
and elsewhere. Later it diverged again, the
spoken form being known to us as Popular
Latin and the written as Low Latin. In
the Middle Ages Popular Latin became
differentiated into the various Romance Languages.

Low Latin and Popular Latin.

As an example of the Romance Languages we shall
take the most familiar to us—French.
Languages descended from Latin are
spoken in the following countries:

History of French.

Italy and Sicily,
Spain,
Portugal,
France, Belgium, and Western Switzerland,
Roumania,
Eastern Switzerland and the Western Tyrol.

The language of Eastern Switzerland is known as
Roumansch or Rhaeto-Romanic[1]. Spanish and Portu-
guese are also spoken throughout South and Central
America, and in parts of the West Indies and of Africa.
These six or more languages are the direct result of the
political ascendancy of Rome.

---

[1] From the Roman province of *Rhaetia*.

Why the language of the Romans has survived in
Gaul and Spain and not in Britain is a
Why do we   difficult question. In each case we have a
not speak
Romance?   Celtic-speaking country occupied for some
centuries by Rome and afterwards invaded
by a less civilised race. Professor Sayce[1] lays it down
as a general rule that "whenever two nations equally
advanced in civilisation are brought into close contact,
the language of the most numerous will prevail. When
however a small body of invaders brings a higher civilisation with them, the converse is more likely to happen."
The Roman conquest of Britain seems an exception to
this rule. But, though it brought a higher civilisation
than it found, and so might have been expected to
establish a Latin dialect permanently, it involved, like
the Norman conquest, no great shifting of population;
it was, in fact, more a military occupation than an im-
migration. In Gaul and Spain, on the other hand, the
natives had a better chance of acquiring the Roman
culture, and Latin had a better chance of establishing
itself among them. For not only did the Roman occupation begin at least a century earlier, but Gaul and, in
a sense, Spain were nearer to the centre of civilisation.
When therefore the later invaders of Gaul and Spain,
such as the Franks, Burgundians, and West-Goths,
entered these countries, they found a higher general
civilisation than the English found in Britain and also
a more firmly established dialect of Latin. It is moreover probable that in the case of Britain the Germanic
invaders bore a somewhat greater proportion numerically
to the conquered race than in the case of Gaul and
Spain.

[1] *Principles of Comparative Philology*, p. 167.

At first these Roman languages, as spoken in the
towns, differed but little from the Popular
Differentia- Latin whence they were derived (see p. 113).
tion of Latin
dialects. In the less Romanised districts the original
Celtic and Iberian died harder, but were
probably extinct by 500 A.D. Meanwhile the Latin
dialects which ousted them gradually diverged from one
another as they became less the official language and
more the language of the people. If we
Parallels in
English. want a parallel to the divergence of Gallic
Latin (or Gallo-Romanic) from Spanish Latin
(or Hispano-Romanic), we should compare the divergence
of English as spoken (1) by descendants of Englishmen
in America and by descendants of Englishmen in
Australia, (2) by two non-English races such as the
African negroes of America and the Chinese. The
English of the American differs from the English of
the Australian, and Negro-English differs from Pidgin-
English; but in the latter case the difference is far
wider. The American Negro's language and the Pidgin-
English of the Far East are the result of non-English
races[1] trying to speak English, whereas American English
and Australian English are mere local varieties of the
same language spoken by the same race in different parts
of the world. The Romance Languages were produced by
these two forms of divergence working together.

Gallo-Romanic is found at an early stage divided into
local dialects. These are classed under two main heads:—

(1) The Langue d'oc of Southern Gaul and North-
Eastern Spain,

---

[1] It is not of course the race which is the important thing here, but
the phonology and grammatical structure of the language originally
spoken by the race.

(2) The Langue d'oïl of Northern and Central Gaul (ousted in the North-Eastern district by Low German, represented nowadays by Flemish).

Oc and *oïl* were the words for 'yes' in the two groups,— *oc* from *hoc*, and *oïl* (modern French *oui*) a compound of *o* (from *hoc*) and *il* (from *illi*). (1) The chief dialects of the Langue d'oc are Gascon, Provençal, and Catalan, the last being the language of Catalonia in Spain. (2) At the time

Norman-French and French of Paris.

of the Norman Conquest of England the Langue d'oïl included among others Norman-French and the French of the Île-de-France, the district round Paris. The former was brought over to England by the Normans; the latter began to influence our language after the accession of Henry of Anjou (see p. 119).

The rise of the Standard Dialect of French, originally

Standard French.

the French of Paris[1], is exactly parallel to the rise of Standard English, originally London English. The necessities of political and commercial intercourse demanded a common dialect, and the dialect of the political and commercial centre became the standard dialect of the country. As with English, however, the other dialects descended from Gallo-Romanic have survived in the spoken language, some of these, e.g. Provençal, having a considerable modern literature.

Our own language belongs to the Western Branch

History of English.

of the Germanic or Teutonic Group. It was probably identical with Frisian at the time

---

[1] Cf. Chaucer, *Prologue to the Canterbury Tales*, l. 124 :

'And Frensh she spak ful faire and fetisly

'After the scole of Stratford atte Bowe,

'For Frensh of Paris was to hir unknowe.'

of the English invasions of Britain, and hence is known at that stage as Anglo-Frisian. It has closer affinities with Dutch and Flemish and Old Saxon than with Modern German, and has therefore been classed with them as the Low[1] German subdivision of Western Germanic.

At the beginning of our era the inhabitants of Britain spoke a Celtic language. The Roman oc-
The Britons.
cupation lasted from the conquest in the first century to the withdrawal of the legions in 411. Though the population of the towns doubtless remained largely Roman or half-Roman, the Romans
Latin
loan-words.
did not succeed in imposing their language upon the Britons as they did upon the Gauls and Spaniards. Traces of their occupation, however, are found in the place-terminations -wick or -wich (uicus) as in Alnwick, Norwich, and -caster, -cester, or -chester (castra) as in Lancaster, Gloucester, Manchester. The other early borrowings from Latin, mile (milia passuum), street (strata uia), wall (uallum), pepper (piper), cheese (caseus), silk (sericum), pound (pondo), mint (moneta), and a few others, came to Britain with the English.

In the 5th century Britain was partially conquered and
The English
Invaders.
settled by the Angles, Saxons, and Jutes, who came from Northern Germany and Southern Denmark. The earliest record of the language,
Beowulf.
the poem Beowulf, may have been composed before the conquest of Britain, when English and Frisian were identical. As the Germanic settlers comprised several distinct tribes it is natural to find varying dialects. These have been placed in four groups :—

[1] So called as belonging to the Lower or more Northern part of the valleys of the Rhine and the Elbe.

(1)   Northern,
(2)   Midland,
(3)   Southern,
(4)   Kentish.

The Northern dialects are represented in literature by
Caedmon, the Southern by Alfred; from
the Midland, modern Standard English[1] is
descended.   Lowland Scotch, the language
of Burns, is a modern representative of Northern English,
which was spoken from the Humber to the Forth.

*Caedmon,
Alfred.*

Except in Wales and Cornwall the Britons were
gradually absorbed by the invading race,
but the modern English words derived from
their language are few and uncertain.   The
best instances are perhaps *dun* (the colour), *mattock*, and
the place-termination *-combe* ('valley') as in *Wycombe*.
A few other Celtic words, e.g. *brat*, came through the
Irish missionaries who settled in Northumbria about 650.

*Celtic Ele-
ments.*

With Christianity in the 7th century came a considerable number of Latin (some originally Greek)
words, especially Church words such as *bishop*
(*episcopus*),*candle*(*candela*),*church*(*κυριακόν*),
devil (*diabolus*), *priest* (*presbyter*), *temple* (*templum*): others
are *lily, pear, sickle, sock, trout*.

*Church-
Latin.*

The Danes or Norsemen, whose incursions began in
the 9th century and who ruled the country,
wholly or in part, from 878 till 1042, brought
a number of Scandinavian words, e.g. *they,
them, their, sister, skin, sky, egg, law, knife, give, take*,
and name-terminations such as the patronymic *-son* as
in *Robinson* and the place-suffixes *-by, -thorp, -thwaite,
-toft*, as in *Whitby, Althorp, Braithwaite, Lowestoft*.

*Scandinavian
Elements.*

[1] i.e. the 'educated' dialect of Southern England.

Norman influence on the language may be said to have begun with the accession of Edward the Confessor in 1042. The Conquest (1066–1071) brought over a Norman aristocracy, speaking a dialect of Old French. From this date the language of the court, the law, and the schools was Norman-French, and English became almost a peasants' dialect. Indeed, though both languages continued to be spoken, the distinction between the two was so marked that more than two centuries passed before English became influenced to any considerable extent by French.

Norman-French Elements.

In 1154 the accession of Henry of Anjou brought the beginnings of a new influence, the literary French of Paris. The contrast between words derived from Norman-French and the importations from Paris-French is seen in the doublets *catch, chase*; *warden, guardian*; *launch, lance*; *wage, gage.* The influence of French has been continued without a break to the present time. Not only have true Old French words like *court, judge, tax, county, rent, sir, captain, army, preach, labour, feeble*, derived mostly from Late Latin, been imported largely into English, but there has been an enormous influx of words taken from Literary Latin by learned Frenchmen. Latin was kept up among scholars throughout the Middle Ages, and even before the Revival of Learning many Latin words came into English through French channels. In the 15th century, especially in the last quarter of it after the introduction of printing, many books were translated into English from French translations. It soon became customary among English scholars to adopt Latin words direct in the forms they would have taken in

French of Paris.

'Learned' French.

'Learned' Latin.

French, and it is now often impossible to distinguish Latin loan-words from Latin-French. Such 'learned' words form nowadays a very large part of the language, and are easily recognisable. A few instances are *captive, scribe, regal, monarch, monument, secure, separate, memory, pious,* and the nouns in *-tion,* such as *nation.*

The supremacy of French as the official and aristocratic language remained unchallenged till about 1250. The first official use of English is found in a proclama-

The London Dialect.

tion of Henry III in 1258. A century later French had practically gone out of use in England. Henry III's proclamation is written in what is known as the London Dialect, which is mainly Midland English but includes some Southern forms.

Wyclif, Chaucer.

It is the language used in the following century by Wyclif and Chaucer, and from 1500 onwards is the only dialect used in writing in England. In Scotland, however, the Northern Dialect remained for some time independent as a written language, and as a spoken language still survives among the lower classes like any other dialect of English. The extension of the London Dialect was due largely to the political centralisation which took place under the earlier Tudors, and the increase of the area over which any speaker of English required to be understood. The introduction of

Tindal.

printing in 1477 and the consequent wider circulation of books, particularly of Tindal's Bible, published between 1526 and 1530, aided greatly in its establishment as the Standard Dialect.

English is generally divided historically into three periods :

Historical Division of English.

(1) the Old English (or Anglo-Saxon) of Caedmon and Alfred ;   (700–1100)

(2) the Middle English

of Wyclif and Chaucer;   (1100–1500)

(3) the Modern English

of Shakspeare, Johnson, and Macaulay;   (1500–1900).

These three periods represent roughly three stages of development, which Sweet[1] sums up as follows:

"Old English may be defined as the period of *full* endings—*mōna, sunne, sunu, stānas*;

"Middle English as the period of *levelled* endings [i.e. endings which have become alike]—*mōne, sunne, sune, stōnes* [all disyllabic];

"Modern English as the period of *lost* endings—*moon, sun, son, stones* = stoṇnz."

The last period may be subdivided thus:—

(i) The Early Modern English

of Shakspeare;   (1500–1650)

(ii) The Later Modern English

of Addison;   (1650–1800)

(iii) Present English.

Of the third, which is the educated speech of London and Southern England (called, in relation to the other dialects, Standard English), we must recognise two great divisions,

(*a*) Spoken or Colloquial,

(*b*) Written or Literary.

In Literary English we employ many words such as *steed, realm, dwell, azure, phantom, might* (= 'strength'), which are never used in conversation except when the speaker employs the mock-heroic style, i.e. speaks the Written Dialect. Literary words are often words which have once been colloquial but have become obsolete. Words otherwise obsolete colloquially are used in proverbs, as *casting pearls before swine* for *throwing pearls in front*

---

[1] *New English Grammar*, Part I. p. 211.

of pigs, and in set phrases like *bite and sup, victuals and drink, goods and chattels.*

We have seen that our language contains foreign elements derived from the following sources:

(1) Popular Latin—

      (*a*) as the result of contact with Rome before the migration to Britain,

      (*b*) as a legacy of the Roman Occupation of Britain;   (4th and 5th Cent.)

(2) Celtic of the Britons, after the English invasions;
                                         (5th and 6th)

(3) Popular Latin, after the introduction of Christianity;   (7th)

(4) Scandinavian, after the Danish invasions;
                                   (10th and 11th)

(5) Norman-French, after the Norman conquest;
                                   (11th and 12th)

(6) Old French of Paris, after the accession of Henry of Anjou;   (12th and 13th)

(7) Literary or Classical Latin—

      (*a*) through 'learned' French; (after about 1300)

      (*b*) direct;   (after about 1450).

Besides these, many words, especially in the Modern English Period, have been adopted from various sources, as commercial enterprise has taken Englishmen further and further afield.

From Low German sources we have, e.g. *deck, skipper, sloop, yacht,* and probably *boy* and *girl*;

from Italian	*balcony, archipelago;*
from Spanish	*sherry, peccadillo, alligator;*
from Portuguese	*binnacle, cocoa;*
from Indian languages	*ginger, sugar;*
from Persian	*chess, peach;*
from the Slavonic Branch	*polka, ukase, vampire.*

From Non-Aryan languages we have, e.g.

from Hebrew	*amen, paschal*;
from Aramaic	*damask, damson*;
from Arabic	*admiral, elixir, algebra, alcohol, cotton, amber*;
from Turkish	*bosh, ottoman*;
from Hungarian	*sabre, hussar*;
from Malay	*amuck, gong,* and probably *orange* and *lemon*;
from Chinese	*tea*;
from Australian	*kangaroo*;
from Polynesian	*taboo*;
from African	*oasis*;
from North American	*toboggan, wigwam*;
from Mexican	*chocolate, tomato*;
from West Indian	*canoe, hurricane, potato*;
from South American	*alpaca, quinine, tapioca.*

It should be understood that many of these words have come into English through other languages, while some, especially names of foreign animals or merchandise, have come direct.

The majority of these loan-words are nouns, but there

English essentially Germanic.

is also a large proportion of adjectives and verbs, especially from Latin and French. In point of structure and inflexion, however, and the simplest and most necessary part of the vocabulary,— the auxiliaries, the pronouns, the numerals, and most of the commonest nouns,—our language is almost entirely Germanic, i.e. it is essentially the language brought over from Lower Germany by the Angles and Saxons.

The student must be careful to distinguish in the

'True' English and adopted words.

following chapters words which are truly English by descent and words which have been adopted from other languages, parti-

cularly as a 'true' English word like *father* and a
borrowed word like *paternal* are often to be traced
ultimately to the same source, though they come into
modern English by totally different channels. Other
instances of this are—

sweet	and *suave*,
feather	and *pen*,
three	and *triple*,
kind	and *gentle*,
frozen	and *frigid*.

Grimm's Law (see Chapter VIII) is concerned only with
the Germanic or true English element in our language.

CHAPTER VI.

CHANGE.

IN the preceding chapter we saw that we have
grounds for believing most European and
some Asiatic languages to have been derived
from one source. Not only do groups of
words meaning 'mother,' 'two,' 'stand,' 'bear,' etc. in the
various languages show striking similarities, but the
history of individual languages from their earliest to their
latest records shows that they have undergone in the lapse

**Facts of
Change.**

of centuries considerable change. Alfred said *mōna* where we say *moon*, Plautus said *faxo* where Cicero said *fecero*, Thucydides said[1] ξύν (ksün) where Demosthenes said

σύν (sün). We have arrived, then, at the

Causes of
Change.

fact that changes in language have taken place; the question now before us is how they have done so.

In spoken language a word may be considered from

Classification
of Changes.

two points of view, its Sound and its Meaning. The phenomena of Change fall under these two heads. The word which Alfred pronounced *mōna* we now pronounce *moon*; to Alfred this word had but one meaning, 'the satellite of the earth,' to us it can have two, (1) 'the satellite of the earth,' (2) any satellite, as 'one of Jupiter's moons.'

A. First, as to Change in *Sound*.

When we speak we experience two kinds

Change in
Sound.

of sensation,

Sensations of
Speech.

(1) we feel the Position of the organs of speech,

(2) we hear the Sound we make.

By repetition we acquire a permanent, though unconscious, mental impression or memory-picture of (1) the Position, (2) the Sound. We also hear other people

Reaction of
Ear upon
Voice.

producing what is intended to be the same sound. This hearing of other people reacts upon the permanent memory-picture already in our minds. Hence, if we go into a new linguistic environment, e.g. from a Scotch to an English school, our pronunciation tends to become assimilated to that of the majority.

---

[1] Or perhaps, more accurately, 'wrote' (see page 99).

Now the number of possible vowel-sounds is theoreti-
Varieties of
Pronunci-
ation. cally indefinite. Hence each vowel, such
as the *a* in *man*, the *ō* in *note*, and the *ā*
in *father*, may be regarded as a class of sounds
varying according to personal or dialectic peculiarities.
Thus the *aw* (ɔ) in *law*, the (o) in *hot*, and the (ā) in *father*,
might be represented thus, each circle of dots indicating
possible pronunciations of the vowel in its centre:—

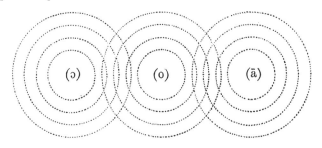

In some speakers the (o)-sound varies in the direction
of *aw* (ɔ), in others in the direction of (ā), e.g. some
pronounce the word written 'dog' somewhat like *dawg*
(dɔg), others somewhat like *dahg* (dāg)[1].

The variation observed in the pronunciation of vowels
has its parallel in that of consonants. But the variation
here is not so marked, the consonant-sounds being acoustically more distinctive.

Everyone knows how differently various speakers, not
Sound-
Change in
Individuals. only of the same community, but of the
same 'dialect-stratum' of the same com-
munity, pronounce what is called the same
sound. More than this, with a little attention we may
notice occasional variations in the same speaker, especially when he is addressing a member of a different

---

[1] A familiar instance is the varying pronunciation of the word *God*.

dialect-stratum. For instance, a shopkeeper uses different pronunciations in speaking (1) to a duchess, (2) to
Isolation.   another shopkeeper, (3) to a tramp. Now
if we may imagine a shopkeeper to cease to
have occasion to speak to anyone but shopkeepers, the
variation in his pronunciation will obviously be greatly
reduced. He will speak in only one of the three ways
he employed before, i.e. a change in his individual pronunciation will have occurred by the *Isolation* of one of
his three varieties of pronunciation. Sound-change may
be observed, then, in the pronunciation of single individuals. It also takes place in the course of the trans-
Imperfect   mission of the language from parents to
Imitation.   children. A child imitates the Sound, not
the Position of the organs required to pro-
duce it, i.e. imitation is acoustic rather than organic.
Consequently his imitation may not be organically
(structurally) correct. To take an instance, a century or
two ago the colloquial pronunciation of *shall not* (*shall*
doubtless being pronounced to rhyme with the French
mal) may have been *shālnt* (sālnt). A child imitating
this might get as near as he could with *shā'n't* (sānt).
If he found this understood, and if neither correction by
his parents nor fear of ridicule made him say *shālnt*, he
would certainly continue to say *shā'n't* as the easier of
the two [1]. By a similar process the word written *know*,
which would not have been so written if the *k* had not
been pronounced, first became (nhōu̯), a breathed *n*, and
then (nōu̯), a voiced *n*, as we pronounce it now. So too
we find *otto* in Italian from the Latin *octo*, γίνομαι in later
Greek for the earlier γίγνομαι, *accedo* and *nosco* in Latin

[1] In reality the *l* probably disappeared before the *o*. Cf. Beaumont
and Fletcher, *Knight of the Burning Pestle*, Act IV. Sc. 5, 'sha'not.'

for *adcedo* and *gnosco*, and in careless colloquial English *reconise* (rekənv̩z) for *recognise*. Laziness and imperfect imitation are responsible for all these changes.

Sound-Changes are classed thus :—

(i) Internal, the changes due (1) to the acoustic qualities of the sound, i.e. the resemblance to the ear of such sounds as *f* and *th* (þ), (2) to the tendencies natural to the organs of speech, e.g. assimilation of a voiced conso-nant to a breathed consonant, and vice versâ (see below),

Subdivision of Sound-Changes.

(ii) External, the changes connected with the ex-pression of ideas.

(i) Instances of Internal Sound-Change are seen in breath and voice assimilation, i.e. if a breathed consonant is combined with a voiced consonant they tend to become either both breathed or both voiced. Thus we pronounce *cats* (kæts) but *dogs* (dogz); similarly *news* is (nyūwz), but *newspaper* (nyūws-peịpə). We may compare in dialectic English *black-bird* pronounced (blægbəd). In the same way the village of Buckden is locally called *Bugden* and was at one time so spelt, while Rushden is known by its inhabitants as (Ruzdn̩) (z̩=s in *measure*). Similar tendencies are seen in combinations of dental (or alveolar) nasals with palatals. Thus we pronounce *come in* (kᴻm in), but *income* is more usually pronounced (iᴻkᴻm) or (iᴻkm̩) than (inkᴻm) or (inkm̩), the alveolar *n* becoming (ᴻ), palatal, before the palatal *k*. Similarly the labiodental *v* in *seven* (sevn̩) tends to change the alveolar (n̩) to the labial (m̩), while the German *lieben* is often pronounced (lībm̩) rather than (lībn̩). Again, *y* (e.g. in *yard*) is a palatal consonant ; hence *s* followed by *y* tends to become *sh* (ṣ), because (ṣ),

Internal.

Assimilation.

E.   9

cerebral, is one step nearer in Place to *y* than *s*, alveolar; hence the pronunciation of *sugar, sure* (ṣugə, ṣūə), for (syugə, syūə). For a like reason the German *ich* is pronounced (iχ), but *ach* (ax).

In this connexion it should be noticed that some

Relative Stability of Sounds.

sounds are naturally less stable, i.e. more liable to change, than others. Thus a Mid Vowel like (ā) in *father* is unstable because it can be modified, according to the adjacent sounds, either backwards to (ō) in *note*, or forwards to (e) in *men*. Long vowels are generally less stable than short, because the longer the sound the more temptation to modify it. From these considerations we should expect the short Front Vowels to be the most stable, and this seems to be the case. The *i* in *wit* is a short Front Vowel and has been preserved from the original Aryan.

External.

(ii) We now come to External Sound-Change. Under this heading come changes which are due to Popular Etymology. It is a matter

Popular Etymology.

of common observation that a word (or phrase) borrowed from a foreign language or for any reason unfamiliar, a word which has no intrinsic or derivative meaning to the speaker, is altered by him to a word that has such a meaning. Thus *asparagus* becomes *sparrow-grass*, and the *rose des quatres saisons* is known to gardeners as the *quarter-sessions rose*. Similarly *haricot veins* for *varicose veins*. In the phrase *to shoot rubbish* we are really employing the French word *chûte*, which has nothing to do with shooting. *Train-oil* has no connexion with railway trains, but is cognate with the German *Träne* 'a tear.' *Sweetheart* is for *sweetard*, the suffix being the same as in *niggard, sluggard, coward*. Somewhat similar is the change of the inn-sign *The*

Bacchanals to *The Bag of Nails*, and others of the same type[1].

The misunderstanding of a phrase will often lead
Misunder-
standing.
to change of form (sound). In *Robinson Crusoe* Defoe speaks of 'paying out the cable to the *better* end,' i.e. as far as it will go; we now speak of the '*bitter* end.'

Sound-Change of all kinds is largely brought about
Mixture of
Races.
by Mixture of Races. In a foreign country, though we may never have seriously studied the language, we can get along very fairly by using the bare stems of words without troubling our-selves with the inflexions. It is a frequent matter for surprise that naturalised foreigners continue to make the simplest grammatical mistakes in English after speaking the language for years. The fact is that words are for communication, and as long as they serve their purpose we are generally content. It is therefore easily intelligible that a large influx of foreigners should give rise to a new simplified dialect of the native language used as a means of communication between the new-comers and the natives. This new dialect would naturally react upon the language spoken by the natives among themselves, and inter-marriage would help to render the changes permanent. This was actually the case with the Danish invasions of England (see p. 118).

We have seen some of the reasons for Sound-Change.
Retarding
Influences.
The next question is, Why do not changes take place so rapidly as to make a language entirely different in the course of a few

[1] Popular Etymology will sometimes, in the case of names and titles, give rise to myths intended to explain them; a familiar instance is Ἀργειφόντης.

generations? It is because working side by side with the
disintegrating tendencies there are conservative tendencies.
Most English children in imitating *three* say *free*. The
reason that *free* does not become the standard pronunciation when the older generation passes away is that the
great majority of speakers with whom the child comes in
contact say *three*, and the pronunciation *free* is not near
enough to *three* to avoid the risks of being misunderstood,
corrected, or ridiculed. Moreover, in this connexion, the
phrase 'the older generation passes away' is misleading.
Generations always overlap. The phrase could only be
accurate here if every human being were married at the
same age and in the same year, produced the same
number of children in the same time, and died at the
same age, as every other human being—and this had
been the case from the beginning[1].

Thus in language, as in politics, there are two great
influences at work, the one reforming, the other conservative. The history of language, or rather, the fact
that there is such a thing as the history of language,
shows that the reforming influence always wins in the
long run. Still, if the disintegration goes
too far in one department, so as to endanger
the fitness of a language to communicate
ideas, there is a conservative reaction in another department. Thus the reforming influence in English has
thrown off most of the Old English inflexions, but the
change is compensated by an increased fixity in the order
of words in a sentence.

Compensa-
tion for dis-
integration.

---

[1] The spelling, too, probably has some influence in checking the
change, though not much. *Sha'n't* was near enough acoustically to
shal'n't or *sha'not* to avoid the above-mentioned risks, yet the spelling
'shall not' has been powerless to check the change.

We may add some further examples of Sound-Change
Further   in English.
Examples.   In Shakspeare we frequently come across
lines like

> *Startles and frights consideration,*

where to preserve the metre we have to pronounce
the suffix *-ation* as three syllables. Shakspeare's ear
-tion   would never have allowed this, unless either
the word had this pronunciation in his time
or had so recently had it as to permit its use in poetry
as an easily intelligible archaism.

In the printed matter appended to drawings by
Leech and others in old numbers of *Punch*,
girl   the 'swell's' pronunciation of *girl* is represented as 'gurl.' This is now pretty generally recognised
as the 'correct' pronunciation, having nearly superseded
the older pronunciation *gairl*. Had *gurl* been the recognised pronunciation in Leech's time, he would have used
the ordinary spelling 'girl.'

In Boswell's *Life*, under the date 1772, Dr Johnson
says that [in 1747] the word *great* was pro-
great, tea   nounced by Lord Chesterfield to rhyme with
state, and by Sir William Yonge to rhyme with *seat*.
Lord Chesterfield's older pronunciation has persisted. But
in *tea* and *sea*, which in 18th century verse are rhymed
with *obey* and *away*, Sir William Yonge's newer pronunciation of *ea* has now become general.

Change in accentuation is seen in comparing the
modern pronunciation with Shakspeare's
Change of accent.   *canónized, revénue, aspéct, perséver,* and
Cowper's *balcóny* in *John Gilpin*. We may
also compare lines of Chaucer like

> *And smalë fowlës maken melodye,*

and   *So priketh hem Natúre in her coráges*[1]
('Then nature excites them in their hearts'). Here we
notice—

    inflexions (*smalë, fowlës, maken, priketh*) now lost or
modified,

    accents (*Natúre, coráges*) now thrown back,

    words now obsolete (*her=their*), or only used colloquially
(*hem ='em*),

    words whose meaning has changed (*priketh, corages*).

    The laws which govern Sound-Change are called
Phonetic Laws, and it is these laws which it

Phonetic Laws. is the chief business of the philologist to
discover. Such a law is Grassmann's that
in Greek and Sanskrit the same syllable cannot both
begin and end with an aspirate (hence θρίξ, τριχός, not
θριχός); or Grimm's Law of the changes of the Stops
between Aryan and the Germanic Group of Languages
(see Chapter VIII.). How far a Phonetic Law is to be
regarded as a Law of Nature, is a disputed point. The
fact that Phonetic Change is to some extent affected by the
human mind seems to put Phonetic Laws beyond the pale
of Natural Law in the strict scientific sense. The Laws
of Chemistry are true always and everywhere, Phonetic
Laws are limited both in time and in area of action.

    B. We now pass on to Changes of *Meaning*.

    The Meaning of a word is the body of associations
called up by it. This is never exactly the

Change of Meaning. same in any two speakers. For instance,

Meaning varies according to (1) the speaker, the word *horse* calls up a different body of
associations to a cab-driver, a veterinary
surgeon, a biologist, and a horse-painter,
respectively. In fact it is with meanings

[1] Prol. *Cant. Tales*, ll. 9, 11.

as with sounds; the meaning of a word is really a class of
meanings varying according to individual and dialectic
peculiarities. The associations in any two cases will be
more or less alike in proportion to the similarity of
education, experience and social environment in the
speakers. More than this, the meaning of
(2) the   a word varies *in the same speaker* accord-
context.
ing to the connexion in which it is used.
When we are shooting, *bird* means a partridge, at an
aviary it means a canary, at a poultry-show a barn-door
fowl. '*Running* a hurdle-race' is a very different thing
to '*running* a flat-race' or '*running* a horse
Isolation of   for a race.' Now, supposing for the moment
Meaning.
that these three are the only uses of the
word *run*, if any two were to go out of fashion owing to
circumstances such as the abolition of hurdle-races and flat-
races, the remaining use would survive as the only use of
the word *run*, or, to put it scientifically, the root-meaning
'run' would have first become extended in three directions
and then been narrowed by *Isolation* in one of these.

We might illustrate the process thus :—

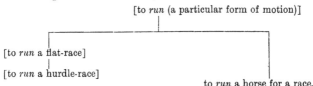

[to *run* (a particular form of motion)]

[to *run* a flat-race]
[to *run* a hurdle-race]
to *run* a horse for a race.

In such a case the transference of meaning would
begin with being occasional, and end with
Occasional   being usual. Such is the history of the
use often
becomes   words *station* in the sense of 'railway-station,'
usual.
station   *stamp* in the sense of 'postage-stamp,' and
stamp   many others. Similarly *wicket* in the sense
wicket   of a small door within a large gate is

practically obsolete in spoken English, while it has survived in its extended use to mean the three stumps at cricket. The same process is going on at the present time in the meaning of the word

motor

motor. From the meaning of 'an engine worked by electricity,' it has come to mean any small engine, and it is now being gradually isolated, in ordinary parlance, in the meaning of 'light mechanical carriage for travelling on roads[1].'

On the other hand, such extensions of meaning as are seen in the use of *leg* to mean one

leg, tail

side of a triangular race-course at sea, or *tail* in the sense of the less valuable members of a cricket team, remain occasional. The last two instances illustrate extension of meaning by Metaphor.

Extension by Metaphor.

A simple example of this may be observed in *I see what you mean*, compared with *I see you.* This form of extension has been discussed already (see p. 8). Words are often isolated in the metaphorical meaning, the original meaning going out

pipe, siege, rascal, friar

of use. Thus *pipe* meant originally a kind of musical instrument; *siege*, a 'seat' or 'sitting down' (Old French); *rascal*, an animal not worth hunting (Middle English); *friar*, a 'brother' (Old French).

The meaning of words, like sounds, has a tendency to change in passing to a new generation. The

Change in transmission to a new generation.

use as well as the pronunciation may be 'incorrectly' (i.e. unlike the majority) imitated. Such 'mistakes' would be to apply the word *congregation* to an audience at a theatre, or the word *nightshirt* to a surplice. These are usually corrected either (1) by parents and others, (2) by ridicule,

[1] There is a more or less distinct implication that the engine is part of the vehicle.

or (3) by risk of being misunderstood. But it is obvious that if a large number of individuals unite in a misapprehension, the new meaning or group of possible meanings will only partially correspond with the meanings attached to the word by the older generation. This is the first step towards change of meaning by Isolation. The following are examples of changes brought about in this way. The word *skirt* was once identi-

skirt

cal with *shirt*, a garment so called because it was *short*; it afterwards came to mean the lower part of such a garment or of any garment (cf. the Authorised Version *the skirts of his clothing*, also the verb *to skirt* and the noun *outskirts*), then a lower garment, and finally a lower feminine garment, which is now the usual meaning.

In Old English *sad*, like the German cognate *satt*, meant 'sated'; in Chaucer it means 'calm,'

sad

'serious'; in Shakspeare 'serious' (cf. 'in good sadness'), 'mournful'; and in the seventeenth century it became isolated in the latter sense.

The original sense of *town* in its Old English form *tūn*, like the German *Zaun*[1], was a piece of

town

enclosed ground; then it came to mean a farm with its buildings; then a village (as still in some dialects); and finally what it means now.

Words are often identical in form (spoken or written or both) with quite different meanings.

Divergence and Convergence.

These have either (1) diverged in meaning or (2) converged in form. Instances of the former are *box, post, crane*. As examples of convergence in form we may notice—

---

[1] In Modern German *Zaun* means 'hedge.'

bear (verb) from Old English *beran,* and *bear* (noun) from Old English *bera,*

sun from Old English *sunne,* and *son* from Old English *sunu,*

sound (= 'noise') from Old French *son,* and *sound* (e.g. *Plymouth Sound*) from Old English *sūnd,*

mean (verb) from Old English *mǣnan,* to 'intend,' *mean* (adjective) from Old English *mǣne,* 'wicked,' and *mean* (noun) from Old French *meyen* (Fr. *moyen*), Latin *medianus.*

We may add *sight, site; father, farther; beach, beech; pail, pale*[1]; *wreck, reck; taper, tapir.*

Sometimes divergence in meaning is accompanied by differentiation in form (sound) or spelling. Thus *of* and *off, to* and *too, person* and *parson,* were once identical, and of the two spellings *insure* and *ensure* the first is generally used in the business sense (*insure against fire*) and the second in the general sense (*ensure success*). Similarly *practise* is used for the verb, *practice* for the noun. Compare also *indite a letter* and *indict a person, O* (vocative) and *Oh* (exclamation), *ton* (weight) and *tun* (capacity). A strange case of divergence of spelling is seen in *Tonbridge* and *Tunbridge Wells.* In *Smith* and *Smyth* (smɐiþ) we have divergence of form (sound) following upon divergence of spelling.

We have shown how, and to some extent why, changes in sound and meaning come about. We have
Analogy.
still to deal with the greatest change-effecting principle of all.

---

[1] In the Eastern Counties educated people make a distinction here; in *pale* the *l* is voiced (peįl), and in *pail* breathed (peįlh) as in French *table.*

The object of speech is the communication of ideas.
Its Cause.   But it is more than this. Of two possible
ways of doing a thing human nature always,
other things being equal, takes the easier. Civilisation
itself consists mainly in the invention and use of easier
ways of doing things. Gesture can communicate ideas,
Speech can communicate them better. Speech, as we saw
in Chapter I, was originally an improvement upon Gesture,
an improvement because it is less laborious. The object of
Speech, then, is not only the communication of ideas, but
the communication of ideas in the least laborious way.
Hence all labour-saving tendencies are natural to language.

If we expressed 'I go' by *eo*
     'he goes' by *bona*
     'we go' by *tum*
    and 'they go' by *cupidinibus*

our language would be difficult for a native to master,
and practically impossible for a foreigner. There would
be no grammar; it would be entirely a matter of vocabulary. Some languages of savage tribes would seem to
approximate to this condition, e.g. in Fijian, *buru* means
'ten cocoanuts,' *koro* 'a hundred cocoanuts,' *selavo* 'a
thousand cocoanuts.' But fortunately this is exceptional.
In the great majority of cases, association of form in a
language goes side by side with association of meaning,
i.e. words that have something in common in meaning
Grammar.   generally have something in common in form.
In fact, every language has a grammar, or
code of laws not only obeyed but created unconsciously by
each individual speaker. In English such laws—or, to use
a slightly different metaphor, habits—are (1) to put -*s* at
the end of a noun to mean 'more than one,' and (2) to
put -*er* at the end of an adjective to mean 'to a greater
degree.' These laws are unconscious generalisations formed

by each individual from masses of phenomena. In the
first example the mass of phenomena is that of the nouns
in English which make their plural in -s; in the second,
that of the adjectives which make their comparative in -er.

Association-
Groups.

These masses of phenomena are really association-groups of sound *plus* meaning. It is
the tendency of all languages to widen these
Association-Groups, that is, to make words which bear
associated meanings assume associated forms. This tendency is called Analogy.

We have called Analogy the greatest change-effecting
principle of all. It is true that in the long run Analogy acts
as a conservative agent in language by securing a certain
degree of regularity in its propagation and continuity,
but in thus promoting uniformity it often destroys existing
words and flexions, and thus more changes are brought
about by Analogy than by any other single principle[1].

Analogy
classified:

(A) Forma-
tive Analogy.

The phenomena of Analogy may be divided into two
classes (A) of Form, and (B) of Syntax.

(A) A good example of the way in
which Analogy levels incongruities of form
(i.e. widens Association-Groups) is seen in
the French verb. The present tense developed thus,
according to the stress-accentuation in Latin:—

ámō	*aim,*
ámās	*aimes,*
ámat	*aime(t),*
amámus	*amons,*
amátis	*amez,*
ámant	*aiment.*

In Modern French, however, *amons, amez* have been

---

[1] Strong, *Hist. of Lang.* (p. 83), to which I am much indebted throughout this chapter.

changed on the analogy of the other persons to *aimons*,
aimez. The same levelling is seen on comparing New
Testament Greek with Attic, e.g.:—

οἶδα	οἶδα,
οἶσθα	οἶδας,
οἶδε(ν)	οἶδε(ν),
ἴσμεν	οἴδαμεν,
ἴστε	οἴδατε,
ἴσᾱσι(ν)	οἴδᾱσι(ν),

where, however, the changes are due to the great number
of verbs which form their Perfects in -α, -ας, -αμεν, κ.τ.λ.
Similarly in Latin *lepōsem*, *honōsem* (nominative *lepōs*,
honōs) became *lepōrem*, *honōrem*, by the
Phonetic Law that *s* (z) between vowels
changed in Latin at a certain period into *r*. By the
beginning of the Silver Age the nominative, in which
the law did not hold good, had become *lepor*, *honor*, on
the analogy of the other cases. Cicero, however, wrote
lepos, *honos*, and similar forms occur in Vergil. In
English, Analogy has nearly succeeded in making all
nouns make their plural in -*s*. Thus the
Old English plural of *bōc*, 'book,' was *bēc*,
just as the plural of *foot* is *feet*; and the plural of
cow in the Authorised Version is *kine*[1]. The numerals
form an Association-Group. Consequently we find them
affecting one another, e.g. ὀκτακόσιοι instead
of ὀκτωκόσιοι, on the analogy of ἑπτακόσιοι,
and *nouem* for *nouen* (cf. *nōn-us* and Eng.
nine) from *decem*. Similarly the Months are associated
in meaning, and hence the form *Octember* occurs, on the
analogy of *September*, *Nouember*, and *December*, though
it did not succeed in establishing itself.

lepos

books, cows

ὀκτακόσιοι
Octember

---

[1] Historically *kine* is a double plural; *kine* represents *ky-en*, *cȳ* in
Old English being the plural of *cū*. In Lowland Scotch *kye* is still used
for *cows*. Cf. *child*, *childer*, *children*.

'Bad Grammar,' as we call it, is often the result of

I'd a' went   Analogy.   Thus we often hear *took* for *taken*

(used also in poetry) and *went* for *gone*, on
the analogy (1) of the verbs which make both the past
tense and the past participle by adding *-ed*, as

> he played,   he had played,
> he looked,   he had looked;

(2) of the verbs which make both in the same way, as

> think...thought...thought,
> seek...sought...sought.

Similarly $\left. \begin{array}{l} my...mine \\ thy...thine \end{array} \right\}$ hence: $\left\{ \begin{array}{l} his—hisn \\ your—yourn. \end{array} \right.$

Large Association-Groups tend to attract to themselves
not only isolated forms (e.g. *kine* becomes *cows*) or the
members of smaller groups (e.g. *brothers* for the older

New in-   *brethren*), but new words in want of inflexion.
flexions: Take the new verb *to motor*.   In forming its
motored.   past tense and participle we go through some
process like this:—

> $\left. \begin{array}{l} walk...walked \\ hasten...hastened \\ erect...erected \\ form...formed \\ \quad \text{etc.} \end{array} \right\}$ hence: *motor—motored.*

Sometimes one hears the verb *to mote*.   This is formed
thus:—

> $\left. \begin{array}{l} fighter \\ seller \\ protector \\ carrier \\ \quad \text{etc.} \end{array} \right\}$ ...'one who $\left\{ \begin{array}{l} \text{fights} \\ \text{sells} \\ \text{protects} \\ \text{carries,'} \\ \quad \text{etc.} \end{array} \right.$

hence:

motor...'one who—motes.'

The analogy here is not quite accurate; if it were, *motor* would mean the chauffeur and not the machine; but compare *boiler, driver* (a golf-club), *cooker* ('cooking-stove'), where by a kind of personification -*er* is used for the instrument not the agent.

This process is exactly parallel to that of the child learning to talk. He says *runned, goed,*

Analogy in children. *maked,* etc., on the analogy of *walked, dressed, whipped,* etc., and *badder, baddest,* on the analogy of *sweeter, taller, sweetest, tallest.* A child, on being asked where his brother was, has been known to say *He's run-rounding the garden.* This is parallel to such forms as ἐκάθευδε, ἤφίετε in Classical

The Greek Augment. Greek. Modern Greek has extended this use, e.g. ἐπροτίμων, ἠνόχλησα. The converse is seen in the Classical διηκόνουν for ἐδιᾱκόνουν from διᾱκονος.

A particular type of Analogy is the Wrong Division of

Wrong Division. Words (i.e. wrong historically). Thus from *pianist, machinist, violinist,* etc., we might gather that -*nist* rather than -*ist* was the termination; hence such forms as *tobacconist.* Similarly in Greek the termina-

tobacconist tion -ίζω (whence English -*ise*) arose from

Μηδίζω a wrong division of such words as ἐλπίζω, where the real division ἐλπίδ-yω is obscured by the change of δy to ζ (cf. Ζεύς from *Dyēу̯s*, whence Latin *Diouis, Iouis*), and thus we find such words as βασανίζω, Μηδίζω, from βάσανος, Μῆδος, and in English such formations as *standardise, Anglicise.*

The same principle has caused in English the forma-

adder, newt tion of *an adder* for *a nadder,* and vice-versâ,

μέρα *a newt* for *an ewt* (or *eft*), and a few others. An interesting parallel is seen in the colloquial Modern Greek μέρα for ἡμέρα, the first syllable being confused with the article.

It must not be supposed that Analogy works only
Analogy in   by majorities. Sometimes, strangely enough,
Pairs of   the bond of association in a group is exact
Words.   opposition in meaning. The group then
consists of but two members, of which one tends to
become partially assimilated to the other. *Male* is from
the French *mâle*, Latin *masculus* diminutive of *mas*;
female is for *femell*, from the French *femelle*, Latin
femella diminutive of *femina*. The popular mind felt the
opposition in meaning to lie in a single syllable as in the
case of *done* and *undone*, *equal* and *unequal*, and made the
rest of the word correspond to mark the connexion. In
Latin the oldest meaning of *diu* was 'by day' (cf. *interdiu*);
this word has changed *nocte* to *noctu*. Similarly in Greek
ἐκποδών is obviously ἐκ ποδῶν, but ἐμποδών has no such
explanation.

(B)[1]   Analogy is scarcely less active in the domain of
Syntactical   Syntax. For instance, it converts predi-
Analogy.   cates into attributes, thus :—

he is good...a good boy ⎫
he is bad...a bad boy   ⎬ hence :
    etc.   etc.   ⎭   *he is good for nothing—*
                             a good-for-nothing boy.

This is closely parallel to the use of the Latin *frugi*,
frugi   which was originally the dative of *frugem*
               with the meaning 'for enjoyment,' 'pleasant,'
'good' (cf. *curae esse, bono esse*), and only used predi-
catively, but was afterwards used as an attribute as well,
e.g. *seruus frugi atque integer*. Cf. Plautus *improbe nili-
que homo*, and the use of *eius modi = talis*. Similarly

---

[1] For Analogy in Accentuation see the next chapter (p. 151).

drunk, ill, well are properly used only as the predicate (*he is drunk*, etc.) but in colloquial English we now hear *a drunk man, an ill person*[1] for *a drunken man, a sick person*, and a man suffering from a bad leg will speak of the other as his *well leg.*

We sometimes hear nowadays the past tense or past participle *wicketkept, housekept.* These words are formed by Analogy thus:—

  wicketkept

$$\left.\begin{array}{l} keeper...kept \\ sleeper...slept \end{array}\right\} \text{hence}: \left\{\begin{array}{l} wicketkeeper—wicketkept \\ housekeeper—housekept. \end{array}\right.$$

In Greek Syntax, Analogy is responsible for the occasional use in Attic of εἰ with the subjunctive and ἐάν with the future indicative. In Herodotus and Lucian we find πρὸ χρόνου τινός in the sense of 'some time before.' This has been changed by Analogy from πρὸ χρόνῳ τινί (i.e. 'before by some time'), just as in Latin *ante die tertio Kalendas Ianuarias* became *ante diem tertium Kal. Ian.*

  πρὸ χρόνου

In English we often say *He is taller than me* instead of *He is taller than I*, giving *than* the construction of a preposition. This has its parallel in *Than whom no greater man existed*, which is reckoned as correct English. Would-be careful speakers have been known to say *like he* as the result of avoiding *as him.* Analogy is mainly responsible for that bugbear of purists the 'split infinitive.' It is formed somehow thus:—

  than, like

  'Split Infinitive.'

$$\left.\begin{array}{l} \textit{It is finished...It is quite finished} \\ \textit{He has finished it...He has quite finished it} \end{array}\right\} \text{hence}:$$
$$\textit{I hope to finish it—I hope to quite finish it.}$$

---

[1] Even Mrs Piozzi in her *Anecdotes of Samuel Johnson* (pub. 1786) speaks of making 'an ill man well.'

This use is doubtless aided largely by the disjunctive use
of *to* in *He ought to, I should like to very much, For 'tis
their nature to*[1], and similar phrases. Syntactically the
split infinitive is no worse than *In the hope of completely
routing the enemy* or even *I said to Tom's friend*, and
is sometimes found in the best contemporary prose[2].
Where do we go now? can strictly be used only of an

Habitual   habitual action, or an action to be done
Present as   according to regulations. It is frequently
Future.   used, however, of an action to be done according to any previous instructions or pre-arranged plan,
and hence by a further extension it is sometimes used
merely as equivalent to *Where shall we go now?* Here
            the Analogy lies rather in the circumstances
sort of
            or context than in the syntax. The col-
loquial use of *sort of* is an interesting case of Analogy,
e.g. :—

He gave us a sort of lecture ⎱ hence: *He sort of lectured us*
He lectured us   ⎰   or *He lectured us, sort of.*

This is exactly parallel to the use of δῆλον ὅτι and πῶς
δοκεῖς in Greek as adverbs. Compare in Latin *nescio
quem hominem* for *hominem, nescio quis*, and Tacitus's
adfertur rumor rapi in castra incertum quem senatorem
(*Hist.* I. 29).

A peculiar type of Syntactical Analogy is that of
Gender. In Latin all names of trees, though by form
they should be mostly masculine, follow the gender of

---

[1] Dr Watts (d. 1748).

[2] I have found it in some of the eighteenth century novels, e.g.
Richardson's *Clarissa*, and Burney's *Evelina*, and in a metrical translation of a Latin quotation in Holland's Pliny (pub. 1601), p. 589, 'Our
land to duly eare.' According to Jespersen *Eng. Lang.* p. 209, it occurs
as early as the 14th century.

arbor. Similarly in French, though *été* (from *aestātem*)

Analogy in Gender.

belongs by form to the group of feminine nouns in *-té* derived from Latin nouns in *-tās*, it belongs by meaning to the group of the four seasons. *Printemps, automne,* and *hiver* being masculine have made *été* masculine.

The last form of Analogy of which we shall speak is

Contami-nation.

that known as Contamination or Blending. This is the confusion of two or more words or phrases, and is seen (1) in words, (2) in Syntax.

(1) (*a*) In the Form of words it is found in such

In Words: (*a*) in Form,

comic coinages as *anecdotage* from *anecdote* plus *dotage*, and *squarson* from *squire* plus *parson.* But it is also soberly employed in such words as *electrocution* (*electric* plus *execution*). Ἀμφορεύς for ἀμφι-φορεύς (ἀμφί plus φέρω), *idolatry* from εἰδωλολατρεία [1], and the Low Latin *senexter* from *sinister* plus *dexter,* are less conscious formations of the same kind. Similarly we find in inscriptions μισθωσάν-τωσαν from μισθωσάτωσαν plus μισθωσάντων.

(*b*) In the Meaning of words we find confusions such

(*b*) in Mean-ing.

as *burthen* 'a load' with the *burden* of a song (Fr. *bourdon*), *burden* being now used for either; in the same way *tenor* (though in this case it is only a matter of spelling) now does duty for both *tenour* meaning 'import,' 'signification,' and *tenor* in music (Ital. *tenore*).

In Syntax.

(2) In Syntax, Contamination is frequently productive of 'bad grammar,' e.g. :—

---

[1] The shortened form originated in Low Latin.

On attempting to extract the ball, the patient began to sink.

She was not one of those who fear to hurt her complexion.

Everyone present took off their hat.

Examples such as these are common in conversation and newspapers, and are sometimes found in literature. One at least became usual, though it is now obsolete. *Farewell* and *Keep thee well* combined to form *Fare thee well*. A good instance of the same thing is seen in Latin in the use of *quisque* and *pars* with a plural verb. This has its parallel in English in such sentences as *A large number were present*. A rapid speaker has been known to say *The band played See the Conquering Hero came*, the past tense *played* changing *comes* to *came*. In Latin the Gerund and Gerundive constructions were sometimes confused, e.g.:—

> *poenas soluendi tempus* ⎫
> *poenarum soluendarum tempus* ⎬

                          hence : *poenarum soluendi tempus.*

The phrase *in potestatem uenire* was so common that in several passages we find confusions such as:—

    quae ne in potestatem quidem populi Romani esset,

                                    Liv. ii. 14.

Compare also cases of attraction such as :—

    urbem, quam statuo, uestra est, Verg. *Aen.* i. 573,

and the 'Subjunctive because Dependent,' e.g.—

    inuitus feci, ut...fratrem eicerem septem annis postquam consul fuisset (for *fuerat*),   Cic. *de Sen.* xii. 42.

In Greek we may compare:—

    ἔλεγον ὅτι πάντων ὧν δέονται πεπραγότες εἶεν (πάντων for πάντα), Xen. *Hell.* i. 4. 2, διεκομίζοντο εὐθὺς ὅθεν ὑπεξέθεντο παῖδας καὶ γυναῖκας (ὅθεν for ἐκεῖθεν οἵ), Thuc. i. 89,

χαρίζεσθαι οἵῳ σοι ἀνδρί (for τοιούτῳ οἷος σύ),

οἴχεται φεύγων ὃν ἦγες μάρτυρα (for μάρτυς),

and the occasional confusion between καίτοι and καίπερ, e.g.:—

καίπερ ἐκεῖνό γε ᾤμην τι εἶναι, Plat. Sym. 219 C, and ἱκανά μοι νομίζω εἰρῆσθαι, καίτοι πολλά γε παραλιπών, Lysias 31. 34[1].

In concluding this brief discussion of the workings of Analogy we cannot do better than quote the words of M. Bréal[2]:—"If unduly pressed, Analogy would make languages too uniform and, in consequence, monotonous and poor. The philologist, the writer, will always, by taste as by profession, be on the side of the vanquished, that is to say of the forms which Analogy threatens to absorb. But it is thanks to Analogy that the child, without learning one after the other all the words of a language, without having to test them one by one, yet attains to mastery over them in a comparatively short time. It is thanks to Analogy that we are sure of being heard, sure of being understood, even if we chance to create a new word. Analogy must therefore be regarded as a primordial condition of all Language. Whether it has been a source of fecundity and clearness, or whether it has been the cause of sterile uniformity, this the individual history of each language alone can teach us."

[1] Cf. also Grenfell and Hunt, *Oxyrhyncus Papyri*, ii. 237. 8. 30.
[2] *Essai de Sémantique*, Eng. Trans. p. 77.

CHAPTER VII.

VOWEL GRADATION.

Origin—The Vowel Scale—Pitch-Ablaut—Levelling by Analogy—
High Grade and Low Grade—Stress-Ablaut—Weak Grade—
Quantitative Ablaut—*Examples:*—(1) *e : o*—(2) *ē : ō*—(3) *ā : ō.*

IF we compare respectively

πείθω, πέποιθα, and ἔπιθον, in Greek,

fīdo, foedus, and *fīdes,* in Latin,

swim, swam, and *swum,* in English,

and *binden, band,* and *gebunden,* in German,

we cannot fail to be struck by the fact that, disregarding
the prefixes and suffixes, we have in each case three
closely related words or three forms of one word. In
the most important part of the words in each case the
consonants remain the same while the vowels vary. The
same phenomenon may be observed in other Aryan
languages. The principle is known as Vowel Gradation,
or, to use the German term, *Ablaut.*

Origin. As to its origin, the most widely ac-
cepted theory is that it is the outcome of
Accentuation.

If we whisper the sound *ee* (i̯i̯) and then the sound
The Vowel *aw* (ɔ), we find that *ee* sounds a higher note
Scale. than *aw.* If we whisper *ah* (ā), an intermediate note is produced. A singer finds difficulty in
singing *ee* on a low note or *aw* on a high note, while
ah, as a useful 'all-round' sound, is the most suitable
(e.g. in the combination *la*) for trying over a tune without singing the words. Considerations such as these

point to the remarkable conclusion that every vowel-sound has (in each individual speaker) a particular musical note or pitch in which it is most easily pronounced. It is possible, therefore, to arrange the vowels in a kind of musical scale. (Tennyson acted on this principle—unconsciously, perhaps—when he coined a word descriptive of the sound of a peal of bells, in the phrase 'The mellow lin-lan-lone of evening bells[1]'; cf. *ding-dong, tick-tack*.) In this way, it is supposed, the original word

Pitch-Ablaut.

b^here, for instance, of level Stress and Pitch, i.e. having neither syllable louder or higher than the other, appears in Greek as φερ* when it bears the Pitch-accent on its first syllable (e.g. φέρω), and as φορ* when it bears it on its second syllable (e.g. φορά) (It should be remembered that a syllable is said to bear the Pitch-accent, when it is uttered at a higher pitch or musical tone than the adjoining syllables.) If we accept

Greek accentuation often irregular,

this theory, we must admit that in Greek, which unlike most of the dead Aryan languages shows by symbols what the Pitch-accent was, there are more exceptions than regularities. Thus γένος is right but γόνος wrong. The same is the case with τέκος and τόκος, φρένα and φρενός, and many other pairs. But when we re-

owing to Analogy.

member the enormous power of Analogy to break down dissimilarities and simplify what is complex, we realise that the great mass of exceptions existing in a single language does not necessarily disprove the rule for the whole family. We may take it, then,

High Grade and Low Grade.

that if the word or syllable bore the Pitch-accent, it appeared in the *e*-form; if it did not, in the *o*-form. These forms are generally known as the High Grade (*e*) and the Low Grade (*o*).

[1] From the song *Far—far—away* in *Demeter and other Poems*.

The third form, having its origin in the *Stress*-accent,

Stress-Ablaut.
Weak Grade.

is known as the Weak Grade. This Grade is supposed to have originated in absence of Stress, and shows the original word or syllable in its weakest or thinnest form.

Thus we have—

| πείθω | πέποιθα | ἔπιθον |
| πατέρα | εὐπάτορα | πατρός. |

We have taken our examples from what is known as the *e : o* series (I). This, for Greek and Latin, is by far the most important.

To this we must add—

II. the *ē : ō* series, exemplified by—

| τίθημι | θωμός | θετός (for θǝτός), |

and III. the *ā : ō* series, seen in—

| φᾱμί (Doric) | φωνή | φαμέν. |

These three Grades, as they involve a change of vowel, are known as Qualitative. The other type of Vowel-Grade, the Quantitative, is merely a matter of Length, e.g.—

| φορά | φώρ |
| πατέρα | πατήρ. |

This is probably the outcome of compensation for a lost syllable, i.e. φώρ represents an original *bʰŏros*, and πατήρ *pǝtĕros*.

In the following additional examples of the Qualitative Grades we include instances from Latin, but these are more obscure than the Greek owing to the greater vowel-changes peculiar to the language (see pp. 41 and 104 ff.).

[Note: for n̥, m̥, l̥, and r̥ see p. 33.]

HIGH	LOW	WEAK

I. THE *e* : *o* SERIES.

(i)　We begin with the simple vowels, -*e*- : -*o*- :—

-*e*-	-*o*-	-[nil]-
$\begin{cases}\lambda\acute{\epsilon}\gamma\omega \\ \textit{lego, legio}\end{cases}$	$\lambda\acute{o}\gamma os,\ \lambda o\gamma\acute{\iota}\zeta o\mu a\iota$ *ē-logium*	
$\begin{cases}\sigma\tau\acute{\epsilon}\gamma\omega,\ \sigma\tau\acute{\epsilon}\gamma\eta,\ \tau\acute{\epsilon}\gamma\eta \\ \textit{tego} \text{ (for } \textit{stego}\text{)}\end{cases}$	*toga*	
$\tau\rho\acute{\epsilon}\pi\omega$	$\tau\rho\acute{o}\pi os$	$\ddot{\epsilon}\tau\rho a\pi o\nu$ (for $\ddot{\epsilon}\tau\underset{r}{\ }\pi o\nu$)[1]
$\begin{cases}\pi\acute{\epsilon}\tau o\mu a\iota,\ \pi\epsilon\tau\epsilon\iota\nu\acute{o}s \\ \ \\ peto,\ penna \text{ (for} \\ \ \ pet\text{-}sna)\end{cases}$	$\pi o\tau\acute{a}o\mu a\iota,\ \pi o\tau\bar{a}\nu\acute{o}s$ (Doric)	$\pi\acute{\iota}\text{-}\pi\tau\omega,\ \pi\tau\epsilon\rho\acute{o}\nu,$ $\dot{\epsilon}\pi\tau\acute{o}\mu\eta\nu$
$\ddot{\epsilon}\chi\omega$ (for $\sigma\acute{\epsilon}\chi\omega$)[2], $\dot{\epsilon}\chi\upsilon\text{-}$ $\rho\acute{o}s$	$\dot{o}\chi\upsilon\rho\acute{o}s$	$\ddot{\epsilon}\sigma\chi o\nu,\ \ddot{\iota}\sigma\chi\omega$ (for $\sigma\acute{\iota}\sigma\chi\omega$), $\sigma\chi o\lambda\acute{\eta}$
$\begin{cases}\ddot{\epsilon}\pi o\mu a\iota(\text{for}\sigma\acute{\epsilon}q^{w}o\mu a\iota)^{3} \\ sequor\end{cases}$	$\dot{o}\pi\bar{a}\delta\acute{o}s$ (for $\sigma o q^{w}\bar{a}\delta os$) *socius*	$\dot{\epsilon}\sigma\pi\acute{o}\mu\eta\nu$
$\begin{cases}\kappa\lambda\acute{\epsilon}\pi\tau\omega \\ clepo\end{cases}$	$\kappa\acute{\epsilon}\text{-}\kappa\lambda o\phi a,\ \kappa\lambda o\pi\acute{\eta}$	$\dot{\epsilon}\kappa\lambda\acute{a}\pi\eta\nu$ (for $\dot{\epsilon}\kappa\underset{l}{\ }\pi\eta\nu$)[1]
$\begin{cases}\pi\acute{\epsilon}\kappa\omega \\ pec\text{-}to,\ pec\text{-}ten\end{cases}$	$\pi\acute{o}\kappa os$	$\kappa\tau\epsilon\nu\acute{o}s$ (for $\pi\kappa\tau\epsilon\nu\acute{o}s$)
$\begin{cases}\pi\lambda\acute{\epsilon}\kappa\omega \\ im\text{-}plico \text{ (for } im\text{-} \\ \ \ pleco),\ plec\text{-}to\end{cases}$	$\pi\lambda o\kappa\acute{\eta},\ \pi\lambda\acute{o}\kappa a\mu os$	$\dot{\epsilon}\pi\lambda\acute{a}\kappa\eta\nu$ (for $\dot{\epsilon}\pi\underset{l}{\ }\kappa\eta\nu$)
$\begin{cases}\dot{\rho}\acute{\epsilon}\pi\omega \text{ (for } w\rho\acute{\epsilon}\pi\omega)^{4} \\ \ \\ repente\end{cases}$	$\dot{\rho}o\pi\acute{\eta},\ \dot{\rho}\acute{o}\pi a\lambda o\nu,\ \dot{a}\nu\tau\acute{\iota}\text{-}$ $\rho\rho o\pi os$ (for -$w\rho o\pi$-)	$\dot{\rho}a\pi\acute{\iota}s$ (for $w\underset{r}{\ }\pi\acute{\iota}s$)

[1] See p. 185.　　[2] See pp. 164, 178.　　[3] See p. 176.　　[4] See p. 183.

HIGH	LOW	WEAK

e : *o* (continued)

-*e*-	-*o*-	-[nil]-
σκέπ-τομαι, σκέπας	σκοπός, σκοπέω	
τρέφω (for θρέφω)[1], θρέμμα	τέ-τροφα, τροφή	ἐτράφην (for ἐθέφην), τάρφος
πέδον, πεδά (Aeol. = μετά), πεζός (for πεδ-*y*ός)[2] pedem	πόδα tri-pudium (for tri-podiom), repudio	ἐπί-βδα ('day after the feast,' for ἐπί-πδα)
ἔτεκον, τέκος	τέ-τοκα, τόκος	τίκτω (for τί-τκω)
στρέφω	στροφή	στραφείς (for στρͅ-φέντς)
τρέχω (for θρέχω)[1]	τροχός	
φέβομαι	φόβος, φοβερός	
φλέγω	φλογός, φλογερός	fulgeo (for flͅgeo)[3], fulgur
ψέγω	ψόγος, ψογερός	
ἕδος, ἕζομαι (for σέδ-*y*ομαι)[2] sedeo	ὁδός solium, solum, solidus[4]	ἵζω (for σί-σδω) sīdo (for si-sdo)

··

[1] See p. 164.   [2] See p. 182.   [3] See p. 185.   [4] See p. 174.

HIGH	LOW	WEAK

$e : o$ (continued)

(ii) Next, the i-diphthongs, -ei- : -oi- :—

-ei-	-oi-	-i-
$\begin{cases}\text{εἴδομαι (for } wεἰδο-\\ μαι, Fείδομαι), εἶδος\end{cases}$	οἶδα (for wοῖδα) $uīdī$ [1]	ἰδεῖν (for wiδεῖν), ἴδρις, ἰδέα $uideo$
$\begin{cases}λείπω\\ līqui\end{cases}$	λέ-λοιπα, λοιπός	ἔλιπον re-liquus
στείχω	στοῖχος	στίχος
$\begin{cases}πείθω\\ \\ fīdo, fīdus\end{cases}$	πέ-ποιθα foedus	ἔπιθον, πιθανός, πισ- τός (for πιθ-τός) fidēs, fidēlis
ἀείδω (for ἀweίδω)	ἀοιδός (for ἀwοιδός)	
$\begin{cases}λείβω\\ lībo\end{cases}$	λοιβή	λιβάς
$\begin{cases}εἶ-μι\\ eo \text{ (for } ei\text{-}o)\end{cases}$	οἶ-μος	ἴ-μεν, εἰσ-ι-τήρια i-ter

....

(iii) Next, the u-diphthongs, -eu- : -ou- :—

-eu-, -ew-	-ou-, -ow-	-u-
ἐλεύθερος, ἐλεύσομαι (for ἐλεύθ-σομαι)	εἰλήλουθα	ἐλήλυθα, ἦλθον (ἤλυ- θον)
κέλευθος	ἀκόλουθος (for σm- κόλουθος) [2]	

---

[1] For Latin $ī$ representing oi after $u(w)$, cf. οἶκος, $uicus$.　　　[2] See p. 184.

HIGH	LOW	WEAK
e : *o* (continued)		
-*eu*-, -*ew*-	-*ou*-, -*ow*-	-*u*-
{ σπεύδω	σπουδή	
{		*studeo* [1]
{ φεύγω		ἔφυγον, φυγή
{ *fūgi*		*fugio, fuga*
ζεά (for ζεωά, ζεϝά)	φυσί-ζοος (for -ζοωος)	
{ πλέω (for πλέϝω,	πλοῦς (for πλόϝος,	πλῦνω (for πλῦν-yω) [2]
{ πλέϝω), πλεύσομαι	πλόϝος), πλοῦτος	
{ *pluit* (for *plewit*)		
πνέω (for πνέϝω,	πνοή (for πνοιϝή,	ποι-πνῦω (for ποι-
πνέϝω), πνεύσομαι	πνοϝή)	-πνῦ-yω) [3]
{ ῥέω (for σρέϝω, σρέ-	εὔ-ρροος (for -σροωος,	ἐρρύη, ῥυτός
{ ϝω) [4], ῥεύσομαι	-σροϝος)	
{ *ruo* (for *srewo*)		*ob-rutus*
σεῦε (for κyέϝε)	σοῦσθε, δορυ-σσόος	συθείς
	(for -κyόϝος) [5]	
χέω (for χέϝω, χέϝω),	χοή (for χοωή, χοϝή)	χυθείς, χύτρα, χύσις
χεῦμα		
{ γεύω (for γεύσ-ω)		
{		*gusto*

....

[1] The Aryan original was apparently *psteu̯dō*.   [2] See p. 183.

[3] For the reduplication ποι-, cf. ποιφύσσω.

[4] Eng. *stream*; the *t* is peculiar to Germanic and Slavonic.

[5] See p. 182.

HIGH	LOW	WEAK

e : o (continued)

(iv) Next, the Labial compounds, *-em-* : *-om-* :—

-em-	-om-	-m-, -m̥-
βρέμω	βρόμος, βροντή (for βρομ-τή)	
{δέμω, δέμας	δόμος *domus*	ἐδέ-δμητο *māteries* (for *dmāt-*)
{νέμω, νέμος *nemus*	νόμος *numerus*	*emo* (for n̥mo)
{τρέμω *tremo*	τρόμος, τρομερός	
{τέμ-νω, τέμενος *tem-plum*	τομή	ἔτε-τμον, τμητός, ἔταμον (for ἔτm̥-ον)
{εἷς (for σέμς) *sem-per*	ὁμός	ἅμα (for σm̥α), ἅπαξ (σm̥-παξ), μία (σμία) *sim-plex* (for sm̥-)

....

(v) Next, the Nasal compounds, *-en-* : *-on-* :—

-en-	-on-	-n-, -n̥-
{μένω *maneo*	μόνος, μόνιμος	μί-μνω
{μένος *Minerua* (*Menerua* Inscrr.), *re-min-iscor*	μέ-μονα, μοῦσα (for μόντ-*ya*) *moneo, me-mini* (for *memoni*)	μέ-μαμεν (for μέμn̥-μεν), αὐτό-ματος (for -μn̥τος), μαίνομαι (μn̥-γομαι), μάντις *mens, com-mentus*

High	Low	Weak

e : o (continued)

-*en*-	-*on*-	-*n*-, -*ṇ*-
{ γενέσθαι, γένος, γενέτωρ genus, genitor, gens	γόνος, γέ-γονα	γέ-γαμεν (for γέγṇμεν), γί-γνομαι, γάμος (for γṇμος) gi-gno, (g)nascor, genius (for gṇ-yos)
{ τείνω (for τέν-yω) teneo, tenus	τόνος	τέ-τακα (for τέτṇκα) tentus (for tṇ-tos)
κτείνω (for κτέν-yω)	ἔκτονα, τεκνο-κτόνος	ἔκτανον (for ἔκτṇον)
{ σπένδω, σπείσομαι (for σπένδ-σομαι)	σπονδή spondeo	
φρένα	εὔ-φρονος, φρονέω	φρασί, Pindar (for φρṇσί)
πένθος, πείσομαι (for πένθ-σομαι)	πέ-πονθα	ἔπαθον (for ἔπṇθον), πάσχω (for πṇθ-σκω)
{ κεντέω, κέντρον cento ('patchwork')	κοντός ('pole') per-contor	
{ dentis	ὀδόντος	ὀδάξ (for ὀδṇτξ, cf. γνύξ)

....

(vi)   Next, the *r*-compounds, -*er*- : -*or*- :—

-*er*-	-*or*-	-*r*-, -*ṛ*-
δέρκομαι	δέ-δορκα, δορκάς	ἔδρακον (for ἔδṛκον), δράκων, ὑπό-δρα (for -δṛκ)

HIGH	LOW	WEAK

e : o (continued)

-er-	-or-	-r-, -r̥-
σπείρω (for σπέρ- yω)¹, σπέρμα	σπόρος	ἐσπάρην (for ἐσπर̥ην) spor-tula (for spr̥-)
τείρω (for τέρ-yω), τέρμα tero, ter-minus	ἔτορον, τορός	τρητός trītus
φέρω, φέρετρον fero	φορά	δί-φρος, φαρέτρα fors, fortuna (for fr̥ts, fr̥tuna)
ἀγείρω(for ἀγέρ-yω), ἀγέρεσθαι	ἀγορά	ἀγρόμενος
μέρος, μείρομαι (for μέρ-yομαι)	μόρα, μοῖρα (for μόρ-ya)	
	μορτός (Callimachus, 'mortal')	βροτός (for μροτός from μर̥τός)², ἄμ- βροτος, μαραίνω (for μर̥-αίνω) mors, morior (for mर̥ts, mर̥-yor)
ἐγείρω (for ἐγέρ-yω)	ἐγρήγορα	ἔγρομαι
φθείρω(for φθέρ-yω)	φθορά	ἐφθάρην (for ἐφθर̥ην)
χείρ, χερός, εὐ-χερής	χορός	μέχρι (for μέτ-χρ-ι)

....

¹ See p. 183.
² ρα in Aeolic became ρο, e.g. ἐροτός=ἐρατός; βροτός is then an Aeolic
form which became general, ousting βρατός which does not occur.

HIGH	LOW	WEAK

e : *o* (continued)

(vii)   And lastly, the *l*-compounds, *-el-* : *-ol-* :—

-el-	-ol-	-l-, -l̥-
στέλλω(for στέλ-yω)	στολή	ἔσταλμαι(for ἔστ̥λμαι), ἐστάλην
{ τέλλω (for q^wέλ-yω) in-quilīnus, colo (for inquelīnos, quelo)	πόλος (for q^wόλος), αἰ-πόλος (for αἰγq^wόλος) colus ('distaff')	περι-πλομένων
{ τελ-αμών	τόλμα, τολμάω tol-ero, te-tuli (for tétoli)	τέ-τλαθι (for τέτλ̥θι), τάλας, ἔτλην, τλητός tollo (for tl̥-no), lātus[1] (for tlātos)
βέλος	βολή	ἐβλήθην, βάλλω (for βλ̥-yω), ἔβαλον
{ πελ-ταστής pello (for pel-no)	pe-puli (for pépoli)	πάλλω (for πλ̥-yω), πάλμη, παλτός pulsus (for pl̥-tos)[2]
μέλλω (for μέλ-yω)[3]	ἔμολον, αὐτό-μολος	βλώσκω (for μλώσκω)

Of the two remaining Qualitative series there are comparatively few examples.

II.   THE ē : ō SERIES.

-ē-	-ō-	-ə-
ῥήγ-νυμι	ἔρρωγα	ῥαγείς
ἀρήγω	ἀρωγός	

[1] Used as participle of *fero*; *lātus*, 'broad,' is a different word.

[2] The *s* instead of *t* in such forms appears on the analogy of words like *uorsus*, where it represents *tt* (*uort-tos*) by a Latin phonetic law.

[3] See p. 183.

HIGH	LOW	WEAK

ē̆ : ō̆ (continued)

-ē̆-	-ō̆-	-ə-
ἵημι (for σί-σημι), ἧμα *sē-men*	ἀφ-έωκα (for -σέσωκα)	ἑτός (for σα-τός) *sa-tus*
χῆρος *hēres*	χωρίς, χώρα	χατέω, χάζω
τί-θημι (for θί-θημι), θή-κη *fē-ci*	θω-μός	θε-τός (for θα-τός) *fa-cio*

III. THE ā̆ : ō̆ SERIES.

-ā̆-	-ō̆-	-ə-
ἔπτᾱν (Doric)	πέ-πτωκε	
ἔβᾱν (Dor.)	βω-μός	
ἵστᾰμι (for σί-στᾱμι), στᾰ́-μων (Dor.) *stā-men*		στά-σις, στα-τός *sta-tus, sta-tim*
rādo	*rōdo*	
gnā-rus (for gnā-sos), *narro*	γνώ-μη, γι-γνώ-σκω gnō-sco, *ignōro* (for in-gnō-so)	
πτήσσω (Attic, for πτᾱ́κ-yω)	πτώξ ('hare')	ἔπτακον
nātes	νῶτον	
φᾱ-μί, φᾱ́-μᾱ (Doric) *fā-ma, fā-bula*	φω-νή	φα-μέν, φάτις, φάσκω *fa-teor, fa-cies*

CHAPTER VIII.

GRIMM'S LAW AND THE EXCEPTIONS TO IT.

Jacob Grimm — His Law Tabulated — *Exceptions* — Grassmann's Law—Verner's Law—English Parallels—Other Exceptions—Examples.

IN the chapter on Change we discussed the meaning of the term Phonetic Law. Like the Laws of Nature, such as the Laws of Motion formulated by Newton, a Phonetic Law is a generalisation from a mass of phenomena (see p. 134). In 1822, after a long comparison of the vocabularies of Latin, Greek, Gothic, German, English, and other languages, Jacob Grimm formulated his great law of Sound-Change, the law which underlies the different development of the original Stops in Greek and Latin on the one hand and the Germanic languages on the other. For instance, he saw

Greek	Latin	English
δύο	*duo*	*two,*
ποδ-ός	*ped-is*	*foot,*

Jacob Grimm.

and many other groups of more or less obviously kindred words, and comparing other languages arrived at the conclusion that *g* in Greek and Latin appeared as *k* in the Germanic languages, while *d* and *b* in Greek and Latin appeared as *t* and *p* respectively in Germanic. Similarly *k, t, p* are represented in Germanic by *h, th* (þ), and *f* respectively, while Aryan *gʰ, dʰ, bʰ*, which developed differently in Greek and Latin, appear in Germanic as *g, d*, and *b*.

His conclusions.

These changes may be tabulated thus:—

	ARYAN					GERMANIC			
Breathed Stops	k	t	p	become	h¹	þ (*th*)	f		Breathed Spirants
Voiced Stops	g	d	b	become	k	t	p		Breathed Stops
Aspirated Stops	gʰ	dʰ	bʰ	become	g	d	b		Voiced Stops

For our present purpose we may confine our examples to Greek, Latin, and English, the Classical languages generally preserving the original Stop, and our own being the Germanic language most familiar to us. (The vowel-changes of course do not concern us here, but see chapters VII. and IX.)

	PALATAL	DENTAL	LABIAL
ARYAN STOP	k	t	p
GREEK	καρδ-ία	τρεῖς	ποδ-ός
LATIN	cord-is	trēs	ped-is
ENGLISH	heart	three	foot
ARYAN STOP	g	d	b
GREEK	ἀγρ-ός	ποδ-ός	κύβ-ος
LATIN	agr-um	ped-is	—
ENGLISH	acre	foot	heap
ARYAN STOP	gʰ	dʰ	bʰ
GREEK	χήν	τί-θη-μι	φέρ-ω
LATIN	ans-er (*for* hanser)	fa-cio	fer-o
ENGLISH	goose (*Germ.* Gans)	do	bear

¹ For purposes of comparison under Grimm's Law the Aspirate is classed as a Breathed Spirant.

(There would seem to be no very clear example of
Aryan *b* common to all three languages; for Latin and
English cf. *labium, lip,* and for Greek and Latin βάκτρον,
baculum.) It will be seen that Greek and Latin agree
in preserving the Aryan Stop, except in the case of the
Aspirated Stops *gʰ*, *dʰ*, and *bʰ*. These changes are discussed in the next chapter. In comparing φέρω with *fero*
it should be remembered that φ in Classical Attic was not
the same sound as *f*, but (roughly speaking) was a *p*
followed by an *h* as in *uphold.* The changes of Grimm's
Law will be found further exemplified below.

Theoretically there are no exceptions to a Phonetic
Law. Accordingly when certain words were found to
violate Grimm's Law philologists began to look about
Exceptions. for other laws whose action interfered with
it and produced the anomalous forms. The
result of their investigations was the discovery of three
laws, Grassmann's Law, Verner's Law, and the law that
certain combinations are unaffected by Grimm's Law.

(1) Grassmann's Law accounts for such anomalies as:

κιγχάνω	Goth. *gaggan*	Eng. *go* (Scotch
	[pronounced (gaŋan)]	*gang*)
τυφλός		Eng. *dumb*
πίθος		Eng. *body*

Here according to Grimm's Law we should expect the
English words to be *ho, thumb, fody.* Grassmann, however,
comparing ἔχω ἕξω, θρίξ τριχός, and similar pairs, found
that in Greek and Sanskrit a syllable cannot both begin
and end with an aspirate or aspirated Stop, hence

κιγχάνω represents χιγχάνω
τυφλός   „   θυφλός
πίθος   „   φίθος.

(2) Verner's Law explains why in some Germanic
words Aryan *k, t, p* are represented not by *h, þ, f,* but
by *g, d, b.* The best instances (for English) are words
containing Aryan *t,* e.g.:

ἄν-αλτος ('insatiate')	*altus*	*old* (O.E. *eald*)
ἑ-κατ-όν (for -κn̥τ-)[1]	*centum*	*hund-red*
κλυ-τός	*in-clutus*	*loud* (O.E. *hlūd*)
χόρτος	*hortus*	*yard* (O.E. *geard*)
ἄδην (for σάτ-δην,		
Epic ἄδδην)	*satis*	*sad* (see p. 137).

Here Grimm's Law would give us *olth, hunthred, louth,
yarth, sath.* Verner's explanation is that if the preceding vowel in the Aryan word did not bear the
accent, *k, t, p* in Aryan became *g, d, b* in Germanic
instead of *h, þ, f.* In Greek the original accent is sometimes preserved, e.g. ἑκατόν, κλυτός; but this is not
always the case. The anomalies however may be reason-
ably ascribed to Analogy. We have a
similar phenomenon in English in such
pairs as—

Parallel in English.

exáct (igzǽkt)	*éxecute* (éksikyūt)
anxíety (æŋgzéiəti)	*ánxious* (ǽŋksəs)
man-of-wár (mænəvwɔ́)	*whereóf* (wheərɔ́f)[2]
awáy with him (əwéi wið im)	*herewíth* (hiəwíþ),

where, if the preceding vowel does not bear the accent,
the breathed *ks, k, f, þ* become the voiced *gz, g, v, ð,*
respectively.

---

[1] ἑ- for ἁ-, i.e. *sm̥-*, as in ἅ-παξ, *sim-plex,* meaning 'one'; the change
was due to contamination with εἷς, ἑνός, etc., as in ἕτερος for ἄτερος (cf.
θάτερον). See Chapter IX.

[2] This pronunciation is already giving way to (wheəov, hiəwið) on the
analogy of *of, with* in the far more frequent unaccented position.

(3)   The principal exceptions comprised in the third
Law are as follows:—

(i)   Aryan *sk, st, sp* remain unchanged in Germanic,
e.g.:—

ἀστήρ	*star*
στά̄λᾱ (Doric)	*stool*
στόρνῡμι	*strew, straw*
σπείρω	*spread*
σπαρνός	*spare*
σποργίλος (Ar. *Av.* 301)	*sparrow,*

not *sthar, sfread,* etc.

(By a change peculiar to English, Germanic *sk*
becomes *sh* (ṣ), e.g.:—

σκότος	Gothic *skadus*		*shade, shed*
σκάπτω	,,	*skaban*	*shave*
σκῦτος	,,	*skōhs*	*shoe.*)[1]

(ii) In *kt* and *pt* Germanic keeps the *t*, e.g.:—

ὀκτώ	*eight* (O.E. *eahta*)
σκᾶπτον (Doric)	*shaft*

not *eighth* (eiþ), *shafth.*

In the following examples of Grimm's Law and the
exceptions to it, and also in the following chapter, forms
affected by Grassmann's Law are marked [G], by Verner's
Law [V], by the third Law of exceptions [III].

It should be understood that the same word often shows
different stages of the Ablaut in the three languages,
and sometimes, especially in Latin, appears in a nasalised
form (e.g. ὕδωρ, *unda*).

---

[1] *sk* in English is the sign of a borrowed word, e.g. *sky* and *skin*
(Scand.), *school* from Latin *schola*, *screw* from O.F. *escroue* (Fr. *écrou*).
Contrast *ship* (Eng.) with *skipper* (Dutch).

GREEK	LATIN	ENGLISH

k.

ἐπί-κουρος (for -κορ-σος)	curro (for cᵣso, p. 179)	horse
κάλαμος	culmus	haulm ('stalk')
καλέω	calo, Kalendae	hale, haul
κάνναβις	cannabis (from Greek)	hemp (O. E. henep, an early loan-word)
κάπτω, κώπη	capio	haft, heave
κέρας	ceruus, cornu	hart, horn
κίω, κῑνέω	cieo, citus	hie
	clāmo	low (O.E. hlōwan)
κλάζω, κλαγγή	clango	laugh (O.E. hlehhan)
κλέπτω	clepo	shop-lifterᴵᴵᴵ (cf.Goth. hliftus)
κλίνω, κλῖμαξ	in-clīno, clīuus	lean, ladder, Lud-low (O.E. hlǣnan, hlǣder, -hlǣw)
κλυτός	in-clutus	loud ᵛ (O.E. hlūd)
κνήμη, κνημίς		ham (for hanm)
κρῐ-νω	crī-brum, cerno	riddle ('sieve') (O.E. hrĭdder)
κύρτη ('creel')	crātis	hurdle ᵛ
κύτος	cutis	hide ᵛ
κώμη		home, Old-ham (O.E. hām)
κῶνος	cōtis, catus	hone (O.E. hān)
λευκός, λύχνος (for λύξνος)	lūcis, lūceo, lūna (for lūc-sna)	light (O.E. lēoht)
ὀκτώ	octō	eight ᴵᴵᴵ (O.E. eahta)

t.

κρατύς, κάρτα		hard ᵛ
ὀ-δόντος ¹	dentis	tooth (cf.Goth.tunþus)
	mentum	mouth (cf. „ munþs)
πετάννυμι	patulus	fathom ²
τανύ-γλωσσος	tenuis	thin

¹ See p. 188.   ² 'Space covered by the extended arms.'

GREEK	LATIN	ENGLISH
τέκνον, τόκος, τίκτω (for τί-τκω)		*thane* (O.E. þegen, from þīhan 'to grow')
τέρσομαι, τερσαίνω	*terra* (for *tersa*), *tor-reo, ex-torris*	*thirst*
τι-τρώσκω, τέρετρον, τείρω,τρητός,τόρνος	*tero, trītum, terebra*	*thrill* (O.E. þyrlian 'to pierce'), *throw, through*
τήκω (Attic)	*tābes*	*thaw*
τλῆναι, τόλμα, τάλας, τελαμών	*tuli, tollo, lātum* (for *tlātum*)	*thole* ('to endure')
	uentus	*wind* ᵛ (Scand.)

p.

ἀπό	*ap-erio; ab* ᵛ	*off; of* ᵛ (p. 165)
δί-πλαξ, πλέκω	*du-plex, im-plico*	*two-fold, flax*
ἑπτά (for σεπτή)	*septem*	*seven* (O.E. *seofon*)
καρπός	*carpo*	*harvest* (O.E. *hærfest*)
πάομαι	*pānis,pāsco,pābulum*	*food, feed, foster*
παρά, πρίν, πρό,πρός, πρῶτος, πρέσβυς	*prō, prae, prīmus, priscus, pristinus*	*for, from, first, be-fore, for-give, fore-tell*
πατήρ	*pater*	*father* (O.E. *fæder* ᵛ)
παῦ-ρος, παύω	*pau-cus, pau-per*	*few*
πεῖρα, πείρω, πόρος	*perīculum, ex-perior, portus*	*fear, fare, ferry; ford* ᵛ
πενθερός^G('connexion by marriage'), πεῖσ-μα (for φένθσμα) ^G	*offendix* ('band')	*bind, bond, bundle; band* (Scand.)
πέντε (for πένqʷε, p. 175)	*quinque* (for *penque*[1])	*five*[1] (cf. Germ. *fünf*)

[1] Apparently by assimilation of the *p* to the *qu* of the latter syllable; this assimilation may have been assisted by the proximity (in counting) of *quattuor*. The second *f* in O.E. *fīf* (instead of *h*, see p. 175) is also due to assimilation. For Assimilation see p. 129. For the change of *e* to *i* before *w* in Latin, cf. τέγγω, *tinguo*, and *sinciput* for *sēwcaput*, i.e. *sēm(i)-caput*; cf. also our pronunciation of *England*.

GREEK	LATIN	ENGLISH
πέρᾱ, περί	per, per-saepe	far (O.E. feor)
πλέω (πλέϝω), πλώω	pluit(forplewit),plōro	flow, flood, fleet
πλίνθος		flint (?)
πολιός, πελιδνός	pullus, pallidus	fallow-deer
πόρκος	porcus	farrow (O.E. fearh)
πῦρ, πυρρός	pūrus	fire
πῶλος	pullus (for p̣lnos)	foal
ὑπέρ[1]	super (s-uper)[1]	over (O.E. ofer)

....

g.

ἀ-μέλγω[2], βουμολγός	mulgeo, mulctra	milk
γελάω, γλήνη, γαλήνη		clean
	gelu	cold, cool
γί-γαρτον ('grape-stone')	grā-num	corn
γιγνώσκω	(g)nōsco	know, can, ken, un-couth
γλύφω	glūbo	cleave (O.E. cleōfan)
γόμφος ('bolt')		comb (O.E. camb)
γόνυ, γνύξ, γωνία	genu	knee (O.E. cneō)
γράφω		carve (O.E. ceorfan)
ἔργον (for ϝέργον), ὄργανον		work (O.E. weorc)
ζεύγ-νυμι (for ʒευγ-), ζυγόν	iungo, iugum, iu-mentum	yoke
μέγας, μείζων (for μέγγων)	magis, maximus	mickle, much (O.E. mycel)
οἴγω, οἴγ-νυμι (for ὀ-ϝίγνυμι[2])		wicket (from Scand. vīkja 'to turn,' through O.Fr.)[3]
ὀ-ρέγω, ὀ-ρεκτός[2]	rego, rectus	reach, rake, right
	sūgo	suck
ὑγιής	uegeo, uegetus, uigil	wake
φώγω		bake

[1] The rough breathing is probably due to a change from u to yu in primitive Greek (for y(i) becoming h in Greek, see p. 180); the s in Latin is all that remained of ex, cf. ἐξύπερθε; Sanskrit upári.

[2] See p. 188.   [3] Cf. Mod. Fr. guichet and O.E. wican 'to give way.'

GREEK	LATIN	ENGLISH

d.

GREEK	LATIN	ENGLISH
ἀ-μαλδύνω ('destroy')	mollis (for mḻdwis)	melt, malt
δάκνω (for δή̣κ-νω),		tongs (O.E. tange)
δάκος, δῆγμα (Attic)		
δάκρυ, δάκρῡμα	lacrima (l for d, p.174)	tear (Goth. tagr ᵛ)
δαμνάω, δμητός (Attic)	domo, dominus	tame
δατέομαι		ted ('to spread mown
		grass'), tad (dial.
		'manure')ᵛ (Scand.)
δέκα (for δέκṃ)	decem	ten (cf. Goth. taihun)
δέμω, δόμος	domus	timber [1]
δένδρον, δένδρεον (for		tree (O.E. treō)
δέν-δρεϝον), δρῦς		
δέρω, δέρμα, δόρυ		tear ('rend')
δῖος (for δίϝ-yos), Διός	Iūpiter (Dyéu-pater,	Tues-day (O.E.
(for Διϝ-ός), Ζεύς	voc.), Ioui (Dyěw-i	Tiwes-dæg)
(for Δyηύ-s), Ζῆν	from Dyēw-i), diem	
(for Δyη̄[w]-μ) [2]	(dyē[w]-m) [2]	
δύναμαι, δύναμις	bonus (for dwenos) [3]	town
ἔδομαι	edo	eat
ἕδος, ἕδρα, ἕζομαι (for	sedeo, sella (for sed-	sit, set, settle ; seat
σέδ-yομαι)	la), sēdes	(Scand.)
καρδία	cordis	heart
κλαδαρός ('frail')	claudus	halt ('lame')
	claudo (for sclaudo)	slot (Dutch, 'bolt')
μέλδω ('melt')		smelt (Scand.)
οἶδα (ϝοῖδα), (ϝ)ἰδεῖν	uideo	wot, wit, wise
ὀ-δόντος (p. 188)	dentis	tooth (cf. Goth. tunþus)
σμερδαλέος	mordeo, morbus (for	smart
	smordwos [3])	
ὕδωρ, ὕδρος ('water-	unda	water, wet, otter
snake')		

[1] For the inserted b, cf. thunder and Germ. Donner, Lat. tono.

[2] Greek shows the Weak Grade diw- as well as the High Grade dyēw- or dyěw-; ēw- in Aryan became ē- before -m; for the changes of dy- see pp. 182—3.

[3] For b representing dw, du, cf. bellum and duellum, bis and δίς.

GREEK	LATIN	ENGLISH

b. [There are comparatively few examples of the history of this sound in these three languages.]

βαίτη ('sheepskin coat')		*pea-jacket* (Dutch, cf. Goth. *paida*)
	labium, lambo	*lip, lap*
	labo ('totter')	*sleep*
	lubricus	*slip, slippery*
κυβ-ιστάω ('tumble')		*hop*
κύβος		*heap*
στέμβω ('shake')		*stamp* [III]
	trabs	*thorp* (Scand.)

g^h. [For the development of g^h, d^h, and b^h in Latin according to position, see p. 175.]

ἀγαθός (Hesychius ἀκαθός, i.e. ἀχαθός[G])		*good*
ἄγχω, ἄγχι	*ango, angor, angustus*	*anger* (Scand.)
θυγάτηρ (for θυχά-τηρ)[G]		*daughter*
κάχληξ ('pebble')		*hail* (O.E. *hagol*)
κιγχ-άνω (for χιγχ-άνω)[G]		*go* (O.E. *gān* for *gangan*, Scot. *gang*)
χαίρω (for χάργуω), χαρά	*hortor*	*yearn* (O.E. *gyrnan*)
χά-σκω, χάος	*hio, hi-sco*	*yawn* (O.E. *gānian*)
χείρ, χερός, εὐχερής	*hir* (O. Lat.)	
χειμών, χειμερινός, δύσ-χιμος, χίμαρος	*hiems, hibernus*[1], *bī-mus* (for *bi-hīmus*)	*gimmer* (dial. 'lamb that has lived one winter')
χθές (for χγές), χθιζός (for χγθσδγός)	*herī* (for *hesī*), *hester-nus*	*yester-day* (O.E. *geos-tra*)

[1] For *heímrinos*; cf. (F)ἐαρινός, *uērnus* (for *uérinos*).

GREEK	LATIN	ENGLISH
χλόη (χλόϜη), χλοερός	*heluus* ('yellow'), *holus* *hostis*	*yellow, yolk* (O.E. *ge-olu, geoleca*), *gold* *guest* (Scand.)

dʰ.

ἄεθλον (ἄ-Ϝεθλον ¹)	*uadis*	*wed*
ἅμαθος (for σάμαθος)		*sand* (for *samd*)
ἄνθραξ (for σέν-θραξ)ᴳ		*cinder* ² (O.E. *sinder*)
ἠΐθεος (ἠ-ϜίθεϜος)	*uiduus, dī-uido*	*widow*
θάνατος (for θϜάνα-τος), θνῄσκω		*dwindle* (O.E. *dwī-nan*)
θαρσέω		*durst, dare*
θέναρ		*den*
θρῶναξ (Lac.)		*drone* (O.E. *drān*)
θυγάτηρ		*daughter*
θῡμός	*fūmus*	*dust* (cf. Germ. *Dunst*, 'vapour')
θύρα	*fores, forum, forus*	*door*
θύω	*suf-fio* ('fumigate')	
μέθυ, μέθη		*mead*
σπάθη		*spade*ᴵᴵᴵ
τί-θημιᴳ, θήκη	*facio, fēci*	*do*

bʰ.

ἀλφός ('leprosy'), ἄλφιτον	*albus* ³	(O.E. *elfetu*, 'swan')
	libet	*love* (O.E. *lufu*)
ἐρέφω, ὄροφος		*rafter*
	flo, flātus, flāmen	*blow* (O.E. *blāwan*), *blast, bladder*
	flōs	*blossom; bloom* (Scand.)

---

¹ See p. 188.   ² Misspelling due to Fr. *cendre* = Latin *cinis*.
³ Cf. *Albion* (Gaulish).

GREEK	LATIN	ENGLISH
	far	*barley*
	fermentum	*barm*
ὀφρύς		*brow*
πῆχυς^G		*bough, bow* (of a ship)
πυθμήν (for φυθμήν)^G	*fundus, funditus*	*bottom* (cf. Germ. *Boden*)
φάραγξ	*frango*	*break*
φηγός (Attic, 'oak')	*fāgus* ('beech')	*beech, book, buck-wheat*
φημί, φήμη (Attic), φωνή, φάτις	*fāri, fāma, fateor, facies*	*ban, banns*
φορκός ('white')		*birch, Her-bert, Bertha*
φρῦνη ('toad')		*brown*
φύρω	*ferueo, defrutum*	*brew, broth*
φύω, φύσις, φῦλή	*fui, futurus, da-bam*	*be, bower, neigh-bour*
φώγω		*bake*

CHAPTER IX.

SOUNDS WHICH HAVE DEVELOPED DIFFERENTLY IN GREEK AND LATIN[1].

Greek -τι- —*Latin* l *for* d—*Aspirated Stops*—*The Velars*—(i) Un-labialised—(ii) Labialised—s—sw- —sy- —*Initial* y—*Final* m—
i̯ *and* u̯—n̥ *and* m̥—l̥ *and* r̥—*The Vowels*—*Contraction*—*Meta-thesis of Quantity*—*Attic* η—*Prothesis*—*Conclusion*.

WE have seen in discussing Grimm's Law that the six Aryan Stops, k, t, p; g, d, b, remain the same in Greek and Latin. The chief exceptions are:—

(1) in Greek, -τι- (in the middle of a word) before another vowel becomes -σι-; e.g. πλούσιος beside πλοῦτος. Cf. French *station*.

(2) in a few Latin words we find l for d; this is possibly a dialectic change. Cf. δάκρυ, *lacrima*; *odor*, *oleo*; *sedeo*, *solium*; δᾱ(ϝ)ήρ, *lēuir*[2]; *mālus* for *mazdos*, Eng. *mast*; *mīles* for *mizdes*, Gk. μισθός, Eng. *meed* (cf. *soldier* from *solidus*, a coin); and the early loan-word *lanista* from δανειστής.

Aspirated Stops. With regard to the Aspirated Stops, gʰ, dʰ, bʰ :—

(1) gʰ becomes χ in Greek and in Latin h initially[3] and (generally) g medially[4]; e.g. χεῖμα, *hiemis*; χῆρος, *hēres*; ἀχηνία, *egēnus*; ἠχή (ϝᾱχά), *uāgītus*.

---

[1] This chapter does not of course pretend to be exhaustive.

[2] *lēuir* for *lēuer* by Popular Etymology from *uir*.

[3] Before r it became f; cf. χόνδρος below.

[4] Under certain circumstances h or lost altogether, e.g. ὄχος (for ϝόχος) and *ueho*, *maior* (for *mahyor*).

(2) d^h becomes θ in Greek, and in Latin f initially, and with a few exceptions d medially[1]; e.g. θύρα, fores; ἤϊθεος (ἠ-ϝίθεϝος), uiduus.

(3) b^h becomes ϕ in Greek, and in Latin f initially and b medially; e.g. φέρω, ferō; ἄμφω, ambō.

The following are additional examples:—

g^h		
χαμαί	humus, homo[2]	bride-groom[2]
χόνδ-ρος ('groats,' for χρόνθρος)^G	frendeo	grind
χορδή	hīra, hīlla (for hīr-la), haru-spex	yarn (O.E. gearn)
φεύγω (for φεύχω)^G, φυγή	fūgi, fugio, fuga	bow (O.E. būgan)

d^h		
θηλή, θῆλυς	fēlis, fēlix, fīlius[3], fēmina, fētus	
θιγεῖν, θιγγάνω	fīgo	
θραύω (for θραύ-σω)	frūstum	
πείθω (for φείθω)^G, πέποιθα, πιθεῖν	fīdus, fīdo, foedus, fides	bidding-prayer[4], bead, beadsman
οὖθαρ	ūber	udder

b^h		
φλύω ('to bubble')	fluo, fluuius, flūmen	
φύλλον (for φύλγον)	folium	blade
ἀφρός (for ṃφρός)	imber (for ṃber)	
νέφος, νεφέλη	nebula, nūbes, nūbo	
ὀμφαλός	umbilīcus, umbo	navel (O.E. nafela)?

There remain the Velar Stops. These apparently had two forms, Labialised and Unlabialised, i.e. with or without a slight $w(\mathring{u})$-sound following them. They are distinguished thus:

Velar Stops.

Breathed	q		q^w	
Voiced	g	g^h	g^w	g^{wh}.

[1] Before and after r it becomes b;—ἐρυθρός, rubrum, red; uerbum, word.
[2] 'Son of the soil'; -groom for -goom, O.E. guma 'man.'
[3] The i instead of $\bar{e}$ is perhaps due to the i in the next syllable.
[4] O.E. biddan 'to pray'; bid 'to command' is a different word.

(i) The *Unlabialised* Velar Stops q, g, and g^h are practically indistinguishable in Greek, Latin, and English from k, g, and g^h [1].

They may be exemplified thus:—

q	καρπός	carpo	harvest (O.E. hærfest)
	κολωνός	collis (for col-nis), celsus, culmen	hill, holm
	κρέας (κρέϝας)	crūdus, cruor	raw (O.E. hreāw)
	ἀγκών, ὄγκος ('barb')	ancus ('bent-armed'), uncus	angle ('to fish')
g	γέρανος	grūs	crane
	γλοιός, γλίσχρος	glūten (ū for oi)	clay
	στιγμή, στίζω	in-stīgo	stick ('stab'), stitch [III]
	στέγω, τέγω	tego, toga	thatch (cf. Scot. thack)
g^h	χανδάνω	pre-hendo	forget; get (Scand.)
	ὀ-μίχλη [2]	mingo	mist (cf. Goth. maih-stus)
	στείχω		stair, stile (O. E. stæger, stigel) [III]
	[before Liquids] glaber (b for d^h)		glad

(ii) The changes of the *Labialised* Velar Stops are too complicated to be given in detail here, the forms they assume in the various languages differing widely according to the adjacent sounds. Certain laws, however, may be gathered from the following examples, e.g.:—

(1) q^w before *o* in Greek becomes π, and before ι and ε, τ.

(2) g^w generally becomes β in Greek and consonantal *u*(w) in Latin.

It should be noted that these laws hold good *entirely* in Attic alone; cf. Ionic κότερος, κῆ for πότερος, πῆ; Aeolic πίς and Thessalian κίς for τίς; and Aeolic πέμπε for πέντε.

[1] Included in this chapter for convenience.   [2] See p. 188.

qʷ	ποδ-απός (for ποδ- ṇqʷός, cf. Lat. prop-inquus)	quod	what (O.E. hwæt)
	ἕπομαι (for σέπομαι)	sequor	see(cf.Goth.saíhwan)[1]
	ὄμμα (for ὄπ-μα), ὄπωπα	oc-ulus	eye (O.E. eáge)
	τίς	quis	
	πέντε	quinque (for penque)[2]	five[2] (cf. Germ. fünf)
	πέσσω (for πέκγω), ἔπεψα, πεπτός	coquo (for quequo)[3]	(Germ. kochen)[4]
	κύκλος		wheel (O. E. hweól, hweowol)
gʷ	βοῦς	bōs (Oscan for true Latin uōs)[5]	cow
	βορά, βρωτήρ, βάρα- θρον	uoro	
	βαίνω (for βάνγω)[6]	uenio[6]	come(cf.Goth. qiman)
	ἀμείβω	mīgro (gr for gʷr)	
	βαρύς	grauis	
	διερός ('nimble,' δ for gʷ)	uireo	
	δελφύς, ἀδελφός, δέλ- φαξ	uulua (by assimila- tion for uolba)[7]	calf
gʷh	θερμός,θέρος(θ for gʷh)	formus	warm
	θείνω (for θένγω), φόνος	de-fendo	
	ἐ-λαχύς[8] (χ for gʷh)	leuis	light (adjective)
	βάλανος (β for gʷh)	glans	
	νεφρός (φ for gʷh)	nebrundines (dial.)	kid-ney (for kidnere)[9]
	νίφα (for σνίφṃ)	nix, niuem, ninguit	snow

---

[1] 'to follow with the eyes.'   [2] See footnote to p. 168.

[3] By assimilation for pequo, cf. quinque, p. 168; popina is borrowed from Oscan or Umbrian.   [4] Eng. cook is borrowed from Latin.

[5] Cf. βίος, uiuus, Osc. biuus (Nom. Plur.).   [6] For gʷm-yō, p. 185.

[7] For the assimilation, cf. bubile for buuile. Galba (Gaulish = 'Fat-paunch,' Suet. Galb., 3) is probably identical.

[8] See p. 188.   [9] Kid is for quith = 'belly.'

E.   12

It is interesting to note that the consonant in Greek changes *in the same word* according to circumstances:

Cf. ποδ-απός   and τίς (cf. *quod* and *quis*),
πόλος   and τέλλω,
περιπλομένων   and περιτελλομένων.

Similarly, but for Analogy, we should have λείπω, λείπεις, λείπει, λείπομεν, λείπετε, λείπουσι (λείπω is for λείϙᵂω, cf. *re-līquit*, *re-liquus*).

Among the remaining consonants that have developed differently in Greek and Latin, the most important are the Spirants *s* and *y* and the Nasal *m*.

s.

Broadly speaking, *s* remains unchanged in Greek and Latin except that—

(i) in Greek, initial *s* becomes *h* (rough breathing)[1], e.g. :—

ἅλς	sal	salt
ἅμα, ὁμός	semel	same
αὐθ-έντης	sontis	sin (cf. Germ. *Sünde*)
ἑλίκη	salix	sallow (the tree)
ἕλκω	sulco	Devonshire *zool*, 'plough' (O.E. *sulh*)
ἵημι (for σί-σημι)	sēmen	sow, seed
μέλδω		smelt (Scand.)
ἑρμηνεύς	sermo	
ἡμέρα		summer
ῦς	sūs	sow

[1] Lost altogether before consonants (e.g. νίφα, snow; ῥέω, stream, pp. 49, 156) except in the combinations σκ-, στ-, σπ- and sometimes σμ-, e.g. σκοπέω, στατός, σπονδή, σμικρός or μικρός.

and (ii) *s* between vowels is lost in Greek¹, and becomes *r* in Latin; e.g. :—

ἕως² (Dor. ἀώς for ἀϝως, ἀύσως)	Aurōra (for Ausōsa)	east
γένους (γένεος for γένεσος)	generis (for geneses)	kin
νυός (for νυσός)	nurus (for nusus)	
ἰός (Ϝιός for Ϝισός)	uīrus (for uīsus)	
μυός (for μυσός)	mūris (for mūses)	mouse
ὦα (for ὦσα)	ōra (for ōsa)	

Contrast also ζέ-ω, ζεσ-τός ; ūr-o, us-tus.

There are a few apparent exceptions in Greek, e.g.
μέσος; but this stands for μέθγος, cf. Hom. μέσσος, Lat.
medius, Eng. *mid*. (The *s* between vowels in such words
as ἔλυσα was preserved or restored on the analogy of
words like ἔκοψα where the verb-stem ended with a consonant.) Some exceptions in Latin, e.g. *miser, caesaries*,
are due to the following *r*; compounds like *praesideo*
were influenced by the simple word (*sedeo*).

With regard to *s* in conjunction with other consonants it should be noticed that in Greek, σ disappeared
medially—with 'compensation' where possible—(1) before
ν and λ (e.g. φαεινός for φαϝεσ-νός ; θραυλός for θραυσ-
λός, cf. θραυσ-τός)³, and (2) after ν and μ (e.g. ἔφηνα for
ἔφαν-σα, ἔνειμα for ἔνεμ-σα). Latin dropped *s* before *n*,
m, and *l*—with compensatory lengthening medially—(e.g.
niuem, snow; *dīnumero*; *mordeo*, smart; *dīmoueo*; *lubricus*,
slippery; *dīluo*), changed *rs* medially to *rr* (e.g. *terra*, τέρ-

¹ In one Greek dialect it becomes *r* as in Latin; Eretrian inscriptions show such forms as παραβαίνωριν for παραβαίνωσιν.

² The rough breathing is transferred to the beginning from the end of
the first syllable, where it was the intermediate stage between *s* and nil.

³ δύσνοος, δύσλυτος, and similar words were felt to be compounds, and
remained unchanged.

σομαι, cf. Att. θάρρος for θάρσος), and gave *nīdus*, *sīdo* for *nisdus*[1], *sisdo*[2]. Cf. also *differo*, *dīiudico*, *trāno*.

It should be noticed that the rough breathing in
sw-, sy-.   Greek represents, besides Aryan *s*, Aryan
                     sw- (*sŭ-*) and *sy-* (*sĭ-*), e.g.:—

ἡδύς (for σϝᾱδύς)	*suāuis* (for *suādwis*)	*sweet*
ἱδρώς (for σϝιδρώς)	*sūdor* (for *suoidor*)	*sweat*
ὑμήν ('membrane,' for	*suo*	*sew*
σγϋμήν)		

In Latin, *swe-* became *so-*, e.g.:—

ὕπνος (Weak Grade)	*soror* (for *suesor*)	(Germ. *Schwester*)[3]
	sopor, *somnus* (for	(O.E. *swefn*, 'a
	suep-)	dream')
	in-solens	*swell*
	sorbus ('service-tree,'	*sword* (cf. Germ.
	b for *d*ʰ)	*Schwert*)

Aryan *y* at the beginning of a word appears in Greek
y.   as ζ[4]. In Aryan, *y* seems to have differed
                     initially from consonant *i* (*ĭ*, see below), cf.
you and ὑμεῖς, not ζυμεῖς. Perhaps *y* was breathed
(*ch* in German *ich*), and *ĭ* voiced (*y* in *you*). For Aryan *y*
initially, cf.:—

ζυγόν	*iugum*	*yoke*
ζέω (for ζέσω), ζεστός		*yeast*
ζύμη ('yeast')	*iūs* ('broth')	

Final *m* in Greek becomes *n*; in Latin it generally
Final *m.*   remained only as a nasalisation of the pre-
                     ceding vowel (see p. 53), e.g.:—

τόν	*is-tum*
τᾱ́ων (Epic, for *tāsōm*)	*is-tārum*
ἄροτρον	*arātrum*

---

[1] Cf. Eng. *nest*.   [2] Identical with ἵζω, see p. 154.
[3] In English, Scand. *systir* has ousted O.E. *sweostor*.
[4] For its pronunciation see p. 47 and footnote.

In discussing the formation of Diphthongs in Chapter II.

i̯ and u̯.   we noticed that some vowels may lose their syllable-forming power, and in fact be used as consonants. The two vowels *i* and *u* were so used in Aryan, and in this capacity are generally written by philologists *i̯* and *u̯*. Previously in this book the symbols *y* and *w* have been used[1], as more familiar. The apparent distinction between *i̯* and *y* in Aryan (see above) now makes it necessary to adopt the symbols more generally used by philologists, *i̯* and *u̯*. But it should be borne in mind that in Latin there was but one sound for *i* used as a consonant, viz. *y* in English *yard*, and but one for *u* used as a consonant, viz. *w* in English *wit* (or more accurately *ou* in French *ouest*), while in Greek, at any rate in Attic of the 4th century, *ι* and *υ* were always true vowels (see p. 50). (When preceded by a vowel, *i̯* and *u̯* form diphthongs in the narrow sense, e.g. *ai̯*, *ou̯*, whose development in Greek and Latin will be noticed shortly.)

(i) When followed by a vowel (in the same syllable) the changes of *i̯* are these:—

	GREEK	LATIN
Initially	*h*	i (*j*)
Medially	(lost)	(lost)

The changes of *u̯* in the same circumstances do not vary:—

ϝ (or lost)[2]	u (*v*)

---

[1] Except in the case of diphthongs, e.g. *ai̯*, *ou̯*, not *ay*, *ow*; this is to avoid confusion with ordinary English spelling.

[2] Always lost in Attic.

These changes may be exemplified thus:—

1̣ ἧπαρ (π for q̌ᵘ)   iecur
ὑάκ-ινθος (for ἰυϜϟκ-)   iuuencus   young
ὥρα, ὥρος (for ἰωρ-)   hornus ('this year's,'   year, yore
                              for ho-ịōrinos)[1]

Cf. also— τιμῶ[2] for τιμά-ịω   ⎱ amo   for amā-ịō
          φιλῶ[2] for φιλέ-ịω   ⎰ moneo for monē-ịō
          δηλῶ[2] for δηλό-ịω   finio for fini-ịō
                                    statuo for statu-ịō

ṷ Ϝόχος, ὄχος   ueho   wain (O.E. wægn)
ὄϜις, ὄϊς   ouis   ewe
ἔλυτρον ('reservoir') uoluo (for ueluo)[3]   wallow
ἔτος   uitulus[4]   wether[4]
ἰτέα   uĩtis, uĩmen   withy
ἐσθής   uestis   wear(cf.Goth.wasjan)
αἰών   aeuum   aye ('always,' O.E. ā
                                         for āwa)
νέος   nouus (for neṷos)[5]   new

(ii) The changes of ị when preceded by a consonant should be mentioned. In Greek the most important are—

(1) the -σσ- or -ττ- resulting from τị-, κị-, or χị-, when medial, e.g.:—

λίσσομαι   for   λίτịομαι, cf. λιτή
ὄσσε   for   ὄκịε (oqᵘịe), cf. oculus
ἐλάσσων   for   ἐλάχịων, cf. ἐλαχύς[6],

and (2) the ζ- resulting from γị- and δị-, e.g.:—

ἁρπάζω   for   ἁρπάγịω, cf. ἅρπαγος
ἐλπίζω   for   ἐλπίδịω, cf. ἐλπίδος.

For the pronunciation of -σσ- and -ζ- see page 47.

[1] ho-, 'this'; cf. hoc.
[2] Another view is that these are later formations on the analogy of φέρω, etc. (where the ω-form is original), ousting τίμāμι, etc., in most dialects; if this is so, the ị was never there.
[3] For Latin ol for el cf. oliuum borrowed from ἔλαιϜον.
[4] Originally 'yearling.'
[5] For Latin ou for eṷ cf. Old Latin touos (tuus) and Hom. τέος (τέϜος).
[6] Initially the corresponding sound is σ; cf. σεῦε and δορυσσόος, p. 156.

It should also be noted that when ἰ is lost after ν and ρ there is 'compensation' in the preceding syllable, e.g. :—

φαίνω	for	φάνιω, cf. ἐφάνην
πλῦνω	for	πλύνιω, cf. πλέ(ϝ)ω [1]
μοῖρα	for	μόρια, cf. μόρα, μέρος
φθείρω	for	φθέριω, cf. φθορά, ἐφθάρην,

and -λἰ- becomes -λλ-, e.g. ἄλλος for ἄλιος, Latin *alius*. Cf. also ἀλήθεια for ἀλήθεσἰα.

In Latin, dἰ initially becomes *i* (*j*), e.g.:—

Iouis for Old Latin *Diouis* (cf. Ζεύς for Δἰηύς = Latin *diūs*[2])

Iānus for Old Latin *Diānus* (cf. *Diāna*, which preserved its ancient form).

With regard to ϝ it should be added that—

(1) in Greek, when ϝ was lost before ρ, the ρ was doubled medially, e.g. (ϝ)ρήγνυμι, ἐρράγην,

(2) τϝ in Greek became initially σ and medially σσ(ττ), e.g. σε for τϝε (cf. Dor. τύ, Lat. *tu*), τέτταρες for qʷέτϝαρες,

(3) in Latin dϝ became *b*, e.g. *bis* for *dϝis* = δίς (but *duo* two syllables), *bellum* for *dϝellum*[3] (as in Old Latin), *morbus* for *mordϝus* (cf. *mordeo*)[4].

In Chapter II. (p. 32) we explained that certain consonants could form syllables like vowels, and were then included with vowels under the name of Sonants. Some

---

[1] πλῦ- is the Weak Grade corresponding to πλεϝ- or πλευ-.

[2] In the phrase *nudius tertius* (*nu* = 'now,' Gk. νυ); cf. also Plaut. *noctuque et diu*; the accusative *diem* = Ζῆν (for Δἰῆμ), and from this the nominative *diēs* came by analogy. See also p. 170.

[3] Connected with *duo*.

[4] The *u* instead of *b* in *suāuis* (for *suādϝis*, cf. ἡδύς, *sweet*) is probably due to the preceding ϝ.

of these sonant consonants, as their development is different in Greek and Latin, must be dealt with here.

$\underset{\circ}{n}$ and $\underset{\circ}{m}$.　　(i) The Sonant Nasals $\underset{\circ}{n}$ and $\underset{\circ}{m}$ develop on parallel lines as follows:—

	GREEK		LATIN
Before $\underset{\cdot}{i}$	$\underset{\circ}{n}$	$a\nu$	en
Before Sonants	$\underset{\circ}{n}$	$a\nu$	en
Otherwise	$\underset{\circ}{n}$	a	en

	GREEK		LATIN
Before $\underset{\cdot}{i}$	$\underset{\circ}{m}$	$a\nu$	en
Before Sonants	$\underset{\circ}{m}$	$a\mu$	em
Otherwise	$\underset{\circ}{m}$	a	em

These changes may be exemplified thus[1] :

$\underset{\circ}{n}$	$\mu a\acute{\iota}\nu o\mu a\iota$ ($\mu\acute{a}\nu\underset{\cdot}{i}o\mu a\iota$ for $\mu\underset{\circ}{n}\underset{\cdot}{i}o\mu a\iota$)		
	$\tau a\nu\acute{\upsilon}$-$\gamma\lambda\omega\sigma\sigma os$ (for $\tau\underset{\circ}{n}\acute{\upsilon}$-)	*tenuis*	*thin*
	$\acute{o}\nu\acute{o}$-$\mu a\tau a$ (for -$\mu\underset{\circ}{n}\tau a$)[2]	*cogno-menta*	
	$\mathring{a}\tau\epsilon\rho$ (for $\sigma\underset{\cdot}{n}\tau\epsilon\rho$)		*sunder* [v]
	$\dot{\epsilon}\lambda\acute{a}\tau\eta$ (for $\dot{\epsilon}\lambda\underset{\cdot}{n}\tau\eta$)	*linter*	*linden* [v]
	$\delta a\sigma\acute{\upsilon}s$ (for $\delta\underset{\circ}{n}\sigma\acute{\upsilon}s$)	*densus*	
	$\kappa a\tau\acute{a}$	*contra*[3]	
	$\dot{a}$-$\delta\acute{a}\mu a\tau os$	*in-domitus* (for *en-*)	*un-tamed*

[1] In Latin *en, em,* have in certain positions undergone further change.

[2] With Greek a for original ($\underset{\circ}{n}$), cf. Bavarian *könna* for Standard German *können* (kön$\underset{\circ}{n}$).

[3] These represent other stages of the Ablaut, see Chapter VII.

[v] by Verner's Law (see p. 165).

m̥	βαίνω (βάνι̯ω for	uenio	come
	g^wm̥i̯ō)		
	ἅμα (for σṃ̔α) ἁ-πλόος	semel, sim-plex	same
	ἀφρός	imber (for ember, cf.	
		simplex above)	
	πόδα	pedem	[foot]
	δέκα	decem	ten (cf. Goth. taíhun)

Cf. also such forms as τετάχαται for τέταχ-νται (cf. λέλυ-νται), ἐλοίατο for ἔλοιντο. Additional examples will be found under Vowel Gradation, pp. 153 ff.

l and r̥.   The Sonant Liquids l̥ and r̥ also need illustration :

	GREEK	LATIN
l̥	αλ, λα	ol (ul)

	GREEK	LATIN
r̥	αρ, ρα	or (ur)

The alternative forms in Greek are probably connected with original accentuation. Latin, under most circumstances, had changed ol to ul by the Augustan period (see pp. 104 ff.). In certain positions (e.g. ol before l) the older form survived. By Stress-weakening (see p. 41) original ŏr became ur, but only when final (-or in words like lepor, honor represents -ōs, see p. 141; in moneor, regor, it was originally -ōr). The following examples will illustrate the above scheme :—

l̥	ἀλέω (for m̥λει̯ω)	molo (for melo)[1]	meal
	βάλλω (for βl̥ι̯ω)	[Cf. βέλος, βολή[1]]	
	ἕλκω[1], ὁλκός[1]	sulcus (for sl̥cos)	zool (p. 178)
	ἔσταλμαι (for ἔστl̥μαι)	[Cf. στέλλω, στολή[1]]	

[1] These represent other stages of the Ablaut, see Chapter VII.

ḷ (continued)

καλύπτω	oc-cultus	hole
μαλακός	mulceo	
παλτός	pulsus (for pḷtos)[1]	
φλέγω[2], φλόγα[2]	fulgeo (for fḷgeo)	
ἀ-μαλδὖνω (for ἀ-	mollis (for mḷduis)	melt, malt
μḷδὗνι̯ω)		
τάλας, τέτλαθι	tollo (for tḷno)	thole ('to endure')
ἐκλάπην (for ἐκḷπην)	[Cf. κλέπτω, κλοπή[2]]	
ṛ ἐφθάρην (for ἐφθṛην)	[Cf. φθείρω, φθορά[2]]	
καρδία	cordis	heart
φέρω[2]	fors (for fṛts)	birth
τάρφος, ἐτράφην (for	[Cf. τρέφω, τροφή[2]]	
θṛφος, ἐθṛφην)[G]		
κέρας	cornu, ceruus[2]	horn, hart
μορτός[2], βροτός (for	mors (for mṛts)	murder, murther
μρατός)[3]		(O.E. morđor)
πράσον (for πṛσον)	porrum (for pṛsom)	
ῥαπίς (for Fṛπίς)	[Cf. ῥέπω, ῥοπή[2]]	

Additional examples will be found under Vowel Gradation, pp. 153 ff.

Broadly speaking, the Aryan Vowels remain unchanged in Greek and Latin. In Latin, however, the strong Stress-accent which prevailed in early times had the effect of 'weakening' the vowels of unstressed syllables (see Chapter III.). The details of this vowel-weakening are too complicated to be dealt with here. The following examples must suffice:

The Vowels.

δόμος	but	dómus
τό (for τόδ)	but	ís-tud
ἔπεο	but	sequere (for séqueso)
λεγόμενοι	but	légiminī
áestimo	but	éxistimo
ágo	but	súbigo.

[1] See p. 160 footnote 2.
[2] These represent other stages of the Ablaut, see Chapter VII.
[G] by Grassmann's Law (see p. 164).
[3] See p. 159 footnote.

There were also some vowel changes in Latin, e.g. *ol* to
ul (see above, p. 185), *oi* to *ū*, which are due to other causes.

The older Latin forms often occur in Inscriptions
(see pp. 104 ff.), e.g.:—

aidilis (aedes, αἶθος) later   *aedilis*
moiros   later   *mūrus* (cf. οἶνος[1], *ūnus*)
feido (πείθω ᴳ)   later   *fīdo,*

and such forms as *fugāī* corresponding to φύγᾳ (φύγᾱι)
are found in the literature of the early Classical period.
It should be noted that *eу̣*, which is preserved in Greek,
has disappeared[2] in Latin, being represented by *ū*, e.g.:—

εὔω (for *eу̣sō*),   *ūrō* (for *ūsō*).

In the case of the Neutral or Indeterminate Vowel (ǝ) in
Aryan, in both Greek and Latin it was at first identified
with *a*, but was afterwards affected in Latin by the Stress-
accent like other vowels.

The original vowel is often obscured in both languages

Contraction.   by Contraction, e.g. τιμῶ for τιμάι̣ω, *amō* for
Metathesis.   *amāi̯o*. Of two long vowels which cannot
Attic η.   contract, the first both in Greek and Latin
Prothesis.   tends to become short, e.g. ἕως for ἠώς (from
ἄυσως), νεῶν for νηϝῶν (cf. *nāuis*), *plĕō* for *plēo* (cf. *plēnus*).

The Metathesis (or Exchange) of Quantity seen in βα-
σιλέως for βασιλῆος is peculiar to Ionic and Attic Greek.

Of Compensatory Lengthening of vowels in both
languages examples will be found above, pp. 179, 183.

It should be mentioned that Attic changed *ā* to η,
except (1) after ρ[3], (2) after another vowel; e.g. μήτηρ,
Doric μά̄τηρ, Latin *māter*; φηγός, Doric φᾱγός, Latin
fāgus; φρά̄τηρ, *frāter*; πρᾱγμα; χώρᾱ; ἰᾱτρός; καρδίᾱ;
γενεά̄.

---

[1] 'ace.'   [2] *neu* for *nĕу̣e* is a 'spurious' diphthong, see p. 55.
[3] κόρη is for κόρϝᾱ, Ionic κούρη (with compensation).

A word should be added as to the Greek phenomenon of Prothesis. Certain words in Greek are found to have developed a short vowel before the initial consonant. The cause of this is doubtful. In some cases it may have been difficulty of pronunciation (cf. French *esprit* from Latin *spiritus*). It occurs invariably before ρ where it represents original *r* and not *sr* or *wr*, and the quality of the added vowel seems to have been determined, or at any rate affected, by the neighbouring sounds. The most usual prothetic vowels are *a* and ε (e.g. ἀνεψιός, *neptis*; ἀμέλγω, *mulgeo*; ἐρυθρός, *ruber*; ἐλαχύς, *leuis*); but *o* and ι also occur (e.g. ὀδόντος, *dentis*; ἴκτις, κτιδέη).

We have now spoken of Language in general and the Study of Language; we have discussed the formation, classification, and representation of Sounds; we have touched on the 'family history' of Greek, Latin, and English; and have dealt with the causes of Change, and its phenomena in the Classical languages. To go further and discuss Words in their Combinations, their inflexions and uses in the individual languages— what, for instance, is the connexion between τρέμουσι and *tremunt*, ναυτῶν and *nautarum*, or why we find Genitive Absolute in Greek and Ablative Absolute in Latin—this is beyond the scope of this book. The remaining chapter might for many reasons have been placed at the beginning. But it was inevitable that the student should find in an account of the history of the subject technicalities which only a perusal of the rest of the book could explain to him. In an elementary work of this nature, to have mixed up the history of the subject with the exposition of it would have been a still greater mistake. It has therefore been thought best to give it as an appendix.

Conclusion.

CHAPTER X.

SKETCH OF THE HISTORY OF COMPARATIVE PHILOLOGY.

Names — Popular Etymology — Beginnings of Etymology — Early Etymology unscientific — Plato's *Cratylus* — Beginnings of Grammar — Aristotle — The Study of Language in the Alexandrian Age—'Analogy' and 'Anomaly'—The Parts of Speech —Dionysius Thrax—τύπτω—Pergamene School—The Stoics— Crates of Mallus—The Study of Language in Italy—Varro— Terminology of Latin Grammar — Probus—Gellius—After the Middle Ages—The Scaligers—Voss—Discovery of Sanskrit— Bopp—Jacob Grimm—Pott—Curtius—Schleicher—Fick—Max Müller—New School—Verner—Grassmann—Whitney—Leskien —Principles of the New School—Paul—Brugmann—Delbrück's *Comparative Syntax*—Bréal's *Sémantique.*

AT a very early stage in his development man doubtless began to take an interest in the meaning of names. When names are first given they are self-explanatory. An epithet signifying an attribute of the person, some physical peculiarity of his or circumstance connected with him, is one day applied to him to distinguish him from other people, and then by imitation becomes permanent. A name is an epithet crystallised. The Roman names *Quintus* and *Strabo*, and the English *Baker* and *Sheepshanks*, are familiar examples. But as time goes on, the special characteristics which the names

originally implied are forgotten. The names descend from
father to son and, as words, become no longer applicable;
or the language to which they once belonged as living
nouns or adjectives pursues its path of development and
leaves them mere labels, unintelligible as words and useful
only 'for purposes of reference.' Thus *Edmund* once meant
'eloquent,' and *Woodward* was a trade-name meaning
'wood-keeper.'

The phenomena of Popular Etymology (see p. 130)
prove that man prefers a self-explanatory
name to a mere label. The same habit of
mind which results in the giving of a self-
explanatory name or nickname, causes him to see meanings
of his own in names whose original meaning is lost to him,
and he will often without knowing it make changes in a
name to make it mean something to him.

*Popular
Etymology.*

Now the difference, as we have said, between a name
and an epithet is a matter of permanence.
We may observe the intermediate stage in
the stock-epithet,—*the briny deep, the green
grass*, οἴνοπα πόντον, *pius Aeneas*. As a rule, these
epithets are not so unintelligible (apart from the person
or thing to which they are applied) as an ordinary name
is. But the tendency to employ them irrespective of the
context marks the beginning of the crystallising process.
It is only to be expected, therefore, that in a race which
has reached the early stage marked by the desire of
making its names mean something, there should be some
minds impelled to go further and inquire into the meaning
of adjectives and common nouns and finally of words in
general. This is the beginning of the science of Etymology.

*Beginnings of
Etymology.*

In its early history, however, Etymology can hardly

claim to be called a science. The foundation of science
Early   is classification, the discovery of common
Etymology   characteristics. It is not enough for the
unscientific.   botanist to collect specimens; he must
classify them according to some system and observe the
regularity which underlies their apparent diversity. Before
it can deserve the name of a science, Etymology must
proceed by some method, and this for a long time it
failed to do. Any superficial resemblance was enough
to establish a derivation, particularly when that derivation
was needed in support of some historical statement or
            philosophical theory. How far Plato's ety-
Plato's   mologies in the *Cratylus*, such as ἄνθρωπος
Cratylus.
            from ὁ ἀναθρῶν ἃ ὄπωπεν, are to be taken
seriously, is not clear. It is generally held that most of
them are parodies of the etymological speculations of the
time. It is with Plato, however, that the study of
language first begins to develop in a new direction, that
of Grammar. In speculation on the origin of language—
the theme of his *Cratylus*—he was preceded by Antis-
thenes and to some extent by Heracleitus and Democritus,
            if not by Pythagoras himself. But in his
Beginnings   works are found the earliest traces of the
of Grammar.
            classification of words into what we call
'parts of speech.' For instance, he distinguishes Subject
(ὄνομα) and Predicate (ῥῆμα) and recognises the dis-
            tinction between Active and Passive. In
Aristotle.
            Aristotle we find the grammatical system
further elaborated. He is the first to distinguish the
Cases (πτώσεις, a word which he also uses for 'Tenses').
In the Alexandrian age of erudition Grammar came
to be investigated first with a view to elucidating the
earlier literature and afterwards as a study in itself.

Plato and Aristotle had regarded the study of language

The Study of Language in the Alexandrian age.

merely as subordinate to dialectic. This was now changed. Zenodotus, the first great critic, compiled an Homeric Glossary; Callimachus wrote on the different names given to the same thing in different nations; Eratosthenes in his work on the Old Comedy dealt with the Attic dialect. Aristophanes of Byzantium not only compiled the first great lexicographical work, in which he traced every word with which he dealt to its original meaning, but also probably

'Analogy' and 'Anomaly.'

wrote a work on 'Analogy' or regularity in grammar, as contrasted with 'Anomaly' or irregularity, in which he drew attention to the rules of inflexion rather than the exceptions. The adherents of these two principles, Analogy and Anomaly, waged a long and bitter war, which continued till the second century A.D. The greatest advance in the study of language in the Alexandrian Period was the definite

The Parts of Speech.

recognition by Aristarchus of eight parts of speech,—Noun (ὄνομα, including Adjectives), Verb (ῥῆμα), Participle (μετοχή), Pronoun (ἀντωνυμία), Article (ἄρθρον), Adverb (ἐπίρρημα), Preposition (πρόθεσις), and Conjunction (σύνδεσμος). One of

Dionysius Thrax. τύπτω.

his pupils was Dionysius Thrax, the author of the earliest Greek Grammar, a book which remained the standard work on the subject for at least thirteen centuries, and is still extant. In it is found our old friend τύπτω; but the complete (and largely fictitious) paradigm of this unfortunate model is not found fully developed till 400 A.D.[1] A grammarian of the school of Dionysius, Tyrannion the

[1] There is an edition by Uhlig, Leipzig, 1883; English Translation by T. Davidson, 1874.

younger, who lived at Rome in the time of Cicero, wrote upon the connexion between the Greek and Latin languages. A contemporary, Didymus Chalcenterus, dealt with names corrupted by change of spelling, and a treatise on letter-changes by Tryphon, who flourished under Augustus, has survived in an abridged form.

Meanwhile Alexandria's literary rival, Pergamum, had been the scene of the labours of the Stoic, Crates of Mallus. The Stoics had long studied grammar and etymology, though only as subsidiary to dialectic. Chrysippus had maintained the cause of 'anomaly' against the adherents of 'analogy,' and Crates continued the struggle. "Crates appears to have regarded all the trouble spent on determining the laws of declension and conjugation as idle and superfluous, and preferred simply to accept the phenomena of language as the arbitrary results of custom and usage[1]." Like modern philologists he seems to have dealt with language as it is, not as it ought to be; but he underestimated the value of investigation into the regularities of grammar. The visit of Crates to Rome about the year 160 did much to establish Greek learning among the Romans.

The Pergamene School.

The Stoics.

Crates of Mallus.

At this point we turn to Italy. Ennius, who died shortly before the visit of Crates, and whose greatest service to posterity was the introduction of the hexameter into Latin, is said to have taken an interest in grammar and spelling. In the next generation the playwright Accius appears to have made some study of orthography (see p. 79). A younger contemporary of his, Stilo, a man of profound

The Study of Language in Italy.

---

[1] Sandys, *Hist. of Classical Scholarship*, p. 155.

learning in both Greek and Latin literature as well as
a great antiquarian, devoted much of his energy to
Grammar and Etymology.   But the earliest existing
Latin work on these subjects is the extant portion of
Varro.   Varro's treatise *de Lingua Latina*, which
          was published before 43 B.C. This treatise,
when entire, dealt with etymology, inflexion, analogy and
anomaly, and syntax.   Varro also wrote upon the origin
of the Latin language.   The chief value of his extant
works for us lies in his quotations from Latin poets whose
works have perished.   The next name is that of Julius
Caesar, who wrote a treatise on grammar in two books,
(1) on the alphabet and words, and (2) on irregularities
in nouns and verbs.   Cicero in his *Orator* attempts
etymologies such as *capsis* from *cape si uis*, and discusses
the pronunciation of *ignoti, ignaui* as *innoti, innaui* and
similar questions, but with him such things are mere
Terminology   side-issues of the study of rhetoric. To the
of Latin   terminology of Latin Grammar, which is the
Grammar.   basis of modern grammatical terminology,
contributions were made by various writers from Varro
to Quintilian.   Thus Varro spoke of the *casus accusandi*,
but called the genitive *casus patricus*.   The Ablative is
said to have been so named by Caesar.   The Declensions
were first distinguished by Palaemon the teacher of
Quintilian.   The foremost grammarian of the first century
Probus.   was Probus, to whom two extant gram-
            matical treatises are ascribed.   He shares
with Palaemon the honour of establishing the main
outlines of the traditional Latin Grammar.   In the next
Gellius.   century the greatest Roman name is that
            of Aulus Gellius, whose *Noctes Atticae* is
largely concerned with Latin lexicography.   He discusses

such questions as the pronunciation of H and V, and whether we should say *curam uestri* or *curam uestrum.* Among Greek authors, the greatest grammarian of this period is Apollonius Dyscolus, the father of Greek Syntax. He is the only ancient grammarian who wrote an independent work on this great branch of grammar. This work is extant, and is remarkable for its scientific treatment of the subject[1].

It is beyond the scope of this book to trace the history of the study of language through the later centuries of the Empire and the Middle Ages. Among many writers, both Greek and Roman, who dealt with this subject, we have noticed a considerable number who wrote on Etymology, and we have seen that there are in ancient literature certain traces of the Comparative Study of Language. But no real advance took place in these departments till quite recent times. Even in the 17th century J. Caesar Scaliger in his treatise *de Causis Linguae Latinae,* bold attempt though it is at independent investigation, shows by such derivations as *pulcher* from πολύχειρ and *ordo* from ὅρον δῶ that he is still groping far from the light. Joseph Scaliger's *Coniectanea ad Varronem* and Voss's *Etymologicum Linguae Latinae* and *Tractatus de Litterarum Permutatione* display some slight advance; but despite the labours of many scholars the era of Modern Comparative Philology cannot be said to begin till the end of the 18th century.

After the Middle Ages.

The Scaligers.

Voss.

Hitherto Latin had been thought to be derived from a dialect of Greek, or Greek and Latin to be cousins both descended from Hebrew. The first step towards the discovery of their

Discovery of Sanskrit.

---

[1] Edited by Schneider and Uhlig, 1878.

true connexion was made in 1786. In that year the oriental scholar Sir William Jones, who was judge of the High Court at Calcutta from 1783 to 1794, introduced the ancient Sanskrit language to European scholars, and by his conception of a great family of languages in which Greek, Latin, and Sanskrit stood side by side became the founder of Modern Comparative Philology. It was thirty years, however, before this great idea was formulated as a valid scientific theory. In 1816 Franz Bopp

Bopp.

published his *System of the Conjugations in Sanskrit in Comparison with those of Greek, Latin, Persian, and German.* This is the first work in which Sir William Jones's idea is supported by a detailed and systematic comparison of the languages. In 1833 Bopp brought out his *Comparative Grammar of Sanskrit, Greek, Latin, Lithuanian, Old Slavonic, Gothic, and German.* The object of this work was to give a description of the original grammatical structure of the languages, to trace their phonetic laws, and to investigate the origin of their grammatical forms. Of these three points Bopp considered the third the most important.

Meanwhile the Germanic languages were being in-vestigated, among others by Jacob Grimm.

Jacob Grimm.

Instead of devoting himself, like Bopp, to grammatical forms, Grimm set himself to study the development of sounds, at the same time confining his researches to a narrower field. Though he made use of Bopp's results published in 1816, there is little doubt that his system was mainly worked out before he knew them. The result of his philological labours was his *German Grammar*, published between 1819 and 1822. In this work he promulgated the law which is known by his name, the Law of the Permutation of Consonants in the Germanic Languages (see p. 162). It is true that the principles embodied in this law had been partly discovered before him by the Danish scholar Rask, but the honour of enuntiating them fully and scientifically rests with Grimm.

The next great name is that of F. A. Pott, whose *Etymological Investigations* appeared between 1833 and 1836. This work, which shows the influence of Grimm, is remarkable as the first really scientific book of derivations.

Pott.

Scholars now began to 'specialise' in the different branches of Aryan philology. Sanskrit, Zend, Slavonic, Lithuanian, and Celtic, each found its investigator. Georg Curtius laboured at Greek; Corssen, Mommsen, and others at the Italic languages. In 1858, in his *Principles of Greek Etymology*, Curtius compared the Greek words with their equivalents in Sanskrit, Zend, Latin, Germanic, Letto-Slavonic, and Celtic, and discussed the sounds and the sound-changes fully and systematically.

Curtius.

In 1861 the history of Comparative Philology begins a new chapter. In that year August Schleicher published his *Compendium of the Comparative Grammar of the Indo-Germanic Languages*. An enormous mass of detail had now been collected by the investigators of the various languages. Schleicher dealt with this as a whole. He assumed for the first time the prehistoric mother-speech of the Aryan Languages, and established a series of laws governing the development of their sounds. He was a follower of Darwin, and all his work is coloured by Darwin's great theory. His attempt to reduce the phenomena of language to conformity with the principles of natural science was not successful, but his premature death in 1868 was a great

Schleicher.

loss to the cause of Comparative Philology. Schleicher's endeavours to reconstruct the Aryan language were con-
Fick.
tinued by August Fick, the first edition of whose *Comparative Dictionary of the Indo-Germanic Languages* was published between 1870
Max Müller.
and 1872. In the meantime Max Müller's *Lectures on the Science of Language* (1861— 1864) had made the results of the scientific investigation accessible to the English public.

Between 1870 and 1879 discoveries were made which
New School.
entirely upset the old theory of the original vowels. It had been supposed that the three simple vowels of Sanskrit and Gothic, *a*, *i*, and *u*, were the only vowels in the original language. The labours of Johannes Schmidt, Osthoff, Ascoli, and particularly Brugmann, proved that this was a mistake. Meanwhile the apparent exceptions to Grimm's Law were removed by further discoveries. In 1875 the Danish scholar, Karl
Verner.
Verner, showed that many of the exceptions
Grassmann.
were due to accentuation in the original language (see p. 165). Others were removed by H. Grassmann's discovery affecting syllables both beginning and ending with an aspirate in Sanskrit and Greek (see p. 164).

These discoveries belong to the New School. In 1867
Whitney.
Professor Whitney in his *Language and the*
Leskien.
Study of Language had given a great impulse to the study of the workings of
Analogy.   In 1878 Professor Leskien of Leipzig and
Principles of   his pupils and adherents, Karl Brugmann,
the New   H. Osthoff, H. Paul, and others, formu-
School.   lated the two great principles of the New
School :

(1) that the laws of Phonetic Change admit of no exception,

(2) that apparent exceptions are produced by Analogy.

The Old School looked upon analogical change with some contempt, as deviating from the laws of phonetic change. The name '*False* Analogy' is a reflexion of this. The Old School in busying itself with such problems as the origin of speech had begun at the wrong end. The New School studied living languages, and the forces which shape and modify them, and argued from them backwards to the dead languages and the history of language in general. For some years a fierce controversy raged between the two schools, but in 1885 with the death of Curtius the Old School ceased to exist. The views of the New School were laid down at greater length by Professor H. Paul in his *Principles of the History of Language*, a work of the greatest value to every student of the subject. But the greatest name in the New School is without doubt that of Karl Brugmann. In his great work *The Elements of the Comparative Grammar of the Indo-Germanic Languages*, published in 1886, he gives a history of the eleven most important languages of the family[1]. This work was supplemented between 1893 and 1897 by Berthold Delbrück's *Comparative Syntax of the Indo-Germanic Languages*. The latter is the result of labours in a new field. Hitherto the forms of words had been studied to the neglect of their functions. This reproach is now being wiped off not only as regards Comparative Syntax but

Paul.
Brugmann.

Delbrück's
Comparative
Syntax.

---

[1] He has recently (1904) published a *Short Comparative Grammar*, to which I am much indebted throughout this book.

also as regards another branch of Comparative Philology,
Semantics or Semasiology. This science is concerned
with tracing the development of the meanings of words.

It is still in its infancy. The foremost
name in connexion with it is that of Professor Michel Bréal of the Collège de France,
whose *Essai de Sémantique*, published in 1897, laid the
foundation of the study.

Bréal's
Sémantique.

LIST OF BOOKS USEFUL TO THE STUDENT OF COMPARATIVE PHILOLOGY.

[Nearly all foreign books in the following list either are to be had in English translations or from their nature do not require translation. For fuller bibliographies the reader is referred to Sonnenschein's *Best Books* and *Reader's Guide.*]

General Works:

Bréal.   *Semantics* (trans.), 1900.

Brugmann[1]. *Elements of the Comparative Grammar of the Indo-
             Germanic Languages* (trans.), 1888—1895, and
             its continuation—

Delbrück. *Vergleichende Syntax der Indogermanischen Sprachen,*
             1893—1900 (not yet translated).

Giles.   *Manual of Comparative Philology,* 1901.

Lubbock (Lord Avebury). *The Origin of Civilisation,* 1902.

Sandys.   *History of Classical Scholarship,* 1903.

Sayce.   *Introduction to the Science of Language,* 1880.

  „   *Principles of Comparative Philology,* 1875.

Strong, Logeman, and Wheeler. *Introduction to the Study of the
             History of Language,* 1891.

Strong.   (Adapted from Paul's *Principien*) *Principles of the
             History of Language,* 1888.

Sweet.   *History of Language* (Dent's Primers), 1901.

Taylor, I. *Origin of the Aryans,* 1892.

Tylor.   *Anthropology,* 1881.

Phonetics:

Behnke.   *Mechanism of the Human Voice,* 1880.

Rippmann. (Adapted from Vietor), *Elements of Phonetics* (Dent's
             Modern Language Series), 1899.

Sweet.   *Primer of Phonetics,* 1902.

[1] His *Short Comparative Grammar* (1904), to which I am much indebted, is not yet translated into English.

202   LIST OF BOOKS USEFUL TO THE STUDENT

The Alphabet:
Clodd.   *Story of the Alphabet* (Newnes' Story Series).
Egbert.   *Introduction to the Study of Latin Inscriptions,* 1896.
Hicks and Hill.   *Manual of Greek Historical Inscriptions,* 1901.
Lindsay.   *Handbook of Latin Inscriptions,* 1897.
Roberts, E. S. *Introduction to Greek Epigraphy,* Part I, 1887.
        Part II, Roberts and Gardner, *Inscriptions of Attica,* 1904.
Thompson, E. M.   *Handbook of Greek and Latin Palaeography,*
            1894.
Whibley.   *Companion to Greek Studies,* 1905.
Encyclopædia Britannica, Supplement, Article 'Writing.'

Greek:
Jannaris.   *Historical Greek Grammar,* 1897.
Prellwitz. *Etymologisches Wörterbuch der Griechischen Sprache,*
            1892.
Purton.   (Translated from Blass) *Pronunciation of Classical
            Greek,* 1890.
Smyth, H. W. *Sounds and Inflexions of the Greek Dialects; Ionic,*
            1894.
Whibley.   *Companion to Greek Studies,* 1905.

Latin:
Bréal and Bailly.   *Dictionnaire Etymologique Latin,* 1885.
Lindsay.   *The Latin Language,* 1894.
    „   *Short Historical Latin Grammar,* 1895.

English:
Bradley.   *The Making of English,* 1904.
Emerson, O. F. *Brief History of the English Language,* 1896.
Greenough and Kittredge. *Words and their Ways in English
            Speech,* 1902.
Jespersen. *The English Language,* 1905.
Kluge and Lutz.   *English Etymology* (Glossary), 1899.
New English Dictionary, 1884—
Skeat.   *Concise Etymological Dictionary of the English
            Language,* 1901.
Sweet.   *History of English Sounds,* 1888.
    „   *New English Grammar,* Part I, 1900.
Toller.   *Outlines of the History of the English Language,* 1900.

French:
Darmesteter. *Historical French Grammar.*

INDEX OF THE PHONETIC SYMBOLS
USED IN THIS BOOK[1].

[Phonetic spelling is indicated by round brackets. Special symbols have not been assigned to such Latin and Greek sounds as differed only slightly from the corresponding English sounds. The differences are pointed out on pp. 47 sqq.]

(a) First element of the diphthong in *how* (haṳ); in many dialects of English the *a* in *pat* is so pronounced, approximating to the *u* (ʀ) in *butt* in Standard English.

(ā) *a* in *father.*

(ʀ) *u* in *butt, o* in *come*, and first element of the diphthong in *high* (hʀi̯).

(æ) *a* in *man.*

(bʰ) *bh* in *abhor* (approximately).

(ɔ) *aw* in *law.*

(dʰ) *dh* in *adhere* (approximately).

(đ̵) *th* in *then.*

(e) (1) *e* in *men*, and first element of the diphthong in *say* (sei̯).
     (2) First element of the diphthong in *fair* (feə).

(ə) The 'Indeterminate Vowel,' employed in many unaccented syllables in English, e.g. the first and last syllables of *together* (təgédə); second element of the diphthong in *fair* (feə).

(ə̄) The long form of the above, heard in *sir* (sə̄), *earth* (ə̄þ).

(gʰ) *gh* in *leg-hit* (approximately).

(g) }
(gʰ) } (see page 26).

---

[1] Certain obvious symbols such as *b, f, k*, have been omitted, as well as others which occur only in the Tables in Chapter II.

(i) *i* in *bit*, and first element of the diphthong in *fear* (fiə).

(ī) First element of the diphthong in *see* (sīi̯).

(i̯) Second element of the diphthongs in *say* (sei̯), *see* (sīi̯), *high* (hɐi̯), and *boy* (boi̯) (see also p. 181).

(kʰ) *kh* in *ink-horn* (approximately).

(l̥) *le* in *table* (tei̯bl̥).

(m̥) *m* in *Yes'm*, *am* in *madam*, *om* in *kingdom*.

(n̥) *en* in *seven*, *on* in season.

(ŋ) *ng* in *sing*, and *n* in *sink*.

(ŋ̊) *'n* in *You c'n go* (yūw kŋ̊ gōy̯).

(ᵚ) In this position, (ŋ) represents the nasalisation of the preceding vowel, e.g. (oᵚ)=*on* in French *son*.

(o) *o* in *not*, and first element of the diphthong in *boy* (boi̯).

(ō) First element of the diphthong in *so* (sōy̯).

(pʰ) *ph* in *top-hat* (approximately).

(q) *q* in *queen*, *c* in *caught*.

(r̥) (see page 33).

(s̬) *sh* in *fish*.

(tʰ) *th* in *at-home* (approximately).

(u) *u* in *put*, *oo* in *foot*.

(ū) *u* in *cruel*.

(y̯) Second element of the diphthongs in *how* (hay̯), *so* (sōy̯) ; (see also page 181).

(x) *ch* in Scotch *loch* and in German *ach*.

(z) *z* in *zeal*, *s* in *raise*.

(z̧) *z* in *azure*, *ge* in *rouge*.

(z̧) as in *As big as Dick* (z̧ big z̧ dik).

(χ) *ch* in German *ich*.

(þ) *th* in *thin*.

GREEK INDEX.

E.　　　　　　　14

210 GREEK INDEX

212   GREEK INDEX

σάπφειρος 103
σβέννυμι 47
σε 183
σέρφος 103
σεῦε 156, 182 note 6
σήρ 104
σήσαμον 103
σίδηρος 102
σίναπι 103
σινδών 103
σισύρα 103
σίω 96
σκ- 178 note
σκᾶπτον 166
σκάπτω 166
σκέπτομαι, σκοπέω, σκοπός 154, 178
   note
σκότος 166
σκυτάλη 63
σκῦτος 166
σμάραγδος 103
σμερδαλέος 170
σμικρός 178 note
σοῦσθε 156
σόφος 95
σπ- 178 note
σπάθη 172
σπαρνός 166
σπείρω 159, 166
σπεκουλάτωρ 46, 104
σπένδω, σπείσομαι 158
σπέρμα 159
σπεύδω 156
σπονδή 158, 178 note
σποργίλος 166
σπουδή 51, 156
-σσ- 99, 182
   ,,   pronunciation of 47
στ- 178 note
στάσις, στατός 161, 178 note
στέγω, στέγη 153, 176
στείχω 155, 176
στέλλω 160, 185
στέμβω 171
στήλη 166
στήμων 161
στιγμή, στίζω 176
στίχος, στοῖχος 155
στολή 160, 185
στόρνυμι 166
στραφείς, στρέφω, στροφή 154
συθείς 156

σύμβολα 63
σύνδεσμος ('Conjunction') 192
σχολή 153

τάλας 168, 186
τανύγλωσσος 167, 184
τάρφος 154, 186
τάων 180
ταῶς 103
τεγγομένας 109
τέγγω 168 note
τέγη 153
τέγω 176
τείνω 158
τείρω 159, 168
τεκνοκτόνος 158
τέκνον 168
τέκος 151, 154
τελαμών 160, 168
τέλλω 160, 178
τέμνω, τέμενος 157
τέος 182 note
τέρετρον 168
τέρμα 159
τέρμινθος 103
τέρσομαι 168, 179
τέτακα 158
τετάχαται 185
τέτλαθι 160, 186
τέτοκα 154
τέτροφα 154
τέτταρες 183
τὴμ πόλιν 48
τίγρις 103
τιθείς 50
τίθημι 152, 161, 163, 172
τίκτω 154, 168
τιμῶ 182, 187
τιρ 96
τίς 177, 178
τιτρώσκω 168
τλῆναι 168
τλητός 160
τμητός 157
τό 186
τόδε and τοδί 7
τοι for οἱ 73
   ,,   for τῷ 73, 75
τόκος 151, 168
τόλμα, τολμάω 160, 168
τομή 157
τόν 180

τόνος 158
τόνς for τούς 96
τόρνος 168
τορός 159
τραπεζίτης 111
τρεῖς 163
τρέμω 157
τρέπω 153
τρέφω 154, 186
τρέχω 154
τρητός 159, 168
τρόμος 157
τρόπος 153
τροφή 154, 186
τροχός 154
τρυτάνη 111
τσίτσικος 8
-ττ- 47, 99, 182
τύ 183
τύπτω 192
τυφλός 164

υ, pronunciation of 49
υ always true vowel in Attic 181
Ψ in early Greek Alphabets 70
ὑάκινθος 182
ὑγιής 169
ὕδρος 170
ὕδωρ 166, 170
υι, pronunciation of 50
υἷς for οἷ 73
ὑμήν 180
υός 50
ὕπατος 104
ὑπέρ 169
ὕπνος 180
ὑπόδρα 158
ὗς 178

φ, pronunciation of 48
Φ absent in early Inscr. 70
Φ in Abu-Simbel Inscr. 72
Φ as a numeral in Latin 77
φαείνος 179
φαίνω 183
φαμέν 161
φάραγξ 173
Φαρνάβαζος 46
φάσηλος 103
φάσκω 161
φάτις 161, 173
φέβομαι 154

φέρετρον 159
φέρω 83, 151, 159, 163, 164, 175, 186
φεύγω 156, 175
φηγός 173, 187
φημή, φημί 161, 173
φήρ 95
φθείρω, φθορά 159, 183, 186
φιλεῖτε 50
φιλῶ 182
φλέγω, φλογός, φλογερός 154, 186
φλοῖσβος 49
φλύω 175
φόβος, φοβερός 154
φοῖνιξ 103
φόνος 177
φορά 151, 159
φορκός 173
φρασί 158
φράτηρ 187
φρένα, φρενός, φρονέω 151, 158
φρύνη 173
ΦΣ for Ψ 71, 74, 75
φυγή 156, 175, 187
φῦκος 103
φυλή 173
φύλλον 175
φύρω 173
φυσίζοος 156
φύσις, φύω 111, 173
φώγω 169, 173
φωνή 161, 173

χ, pronunciation of 48
Χ in early Greek Alphabets 70
Χ for ξ 71, 76
Χ used as numeral in Latin 77
(χ) in German 24, 27
χάζω 161
χαίρω 171
χαλβάνη 103
χανδάνω 176
χάρτης 103
χάσκω, χάος 171
χατέω 161
χεῖμα 174
χειμών, χειμερινός 171
χείρ, χερός, χερσί 159
χεῦμα, χέω 156
χήν 163
χῆρος 161, 174
χθές, χθιζός 171
χίμαρος 171

GENERAL INDEX.

230 GENERAL INDEX

Solon 71, 99
somnus 180
son 121, 138
-son 118
sona for *zona* 78
'Sonants' 32
Sonant Liquids 185
,, Nasals 184
sons 178
sopor 180
sorbus 180
soror 180
sort of 146
sound 138
Sound-Change 126 ff.
Sounds, number of possible 45
South American in English 123
Southern English 118, 120
sow (noun) 178
,, (verb) 178
sp, Aryan 166
spade 172
Spain 114
Spanish 82, 89, 113
,, in English 122
spare 166
sparrow 166
sparrow-grass 130
Speech, *see* Language
Speed of Utterance 5
Spelling 45 ff.
,, , English 59
,, , Influence on Change 132
Spirants 20
,, , Greek 47
,, , Latin 51
'Split' Infinitive 145
spondeo 158
sportula 159
spread 166
squarson 147
st, Aryan 166
Stability of Sounds 130
stair 176
stamen 161
stamp 135, 171
stand 83
Standard English 118, 120, 121
standardise 143
star 166
stare (Lat.) 83
statim 161

station 135
,, (Fr.) 174
statuo 182
status 161
steed 121
stick (verb) 176
stile 176
Stilo 193
stitch 176
'Stock-Epithets' 190
Stoics, Study of Grammar 193
Stone Age 86
stones 121
stool 166
Stops 20
,, , Greek 47
,, , Latin 52
Strabo 189
straw 166
stream 156 *note* 4, 178 *note*
street 117
Stress 5, 37 ff., 42, 105, 107, 140
Stress-Ablaut 152
Stress-Weakening 41, 185, 186
strew 166
Strong Verbs 13
studeo 156
suauis 180, 183 *note* 4
suave (Eng.) 124
subigo 41, 186
'Subjunctive because Dependent'
148
suck 169
sudor 180
suffio 172
sugar 122, 130
sugo 169
sulco 178
sulcus 185
Sumerian 85
summer 178
sun 121
sunder 184
suo 180
super 169
sure 130
sus 178
Swallowing 18
swe-, in Latin 180
sweat 180
Swedes 84
Swedish 91

For EU product safety concerns, contact us at Calle de José Abascal, 56–1°,
28003 Madrid, Spain or eugpsr@cambridge.org.